Pompei

Pompeii

Erich Lessing / Antonio Varone

·TERRAIL·

Cover illustrations

Paquius Proculus and his wife

Fresco in the Fourth Style.
65 x 58 cm. (26 x 23 in.).
House VII, 2, 6, Pompeii.
Naples, Museo Archeologico
Nazionale.

Architectural view with villa

Fresco in the Third Style.
22 x 53 cm. (9 x 21 in.).
Pompeii.
Naples, Museo Archeologico
Nazionale.

Previous page

Architectural view with landscape

Fresco in the early Third Style.
197 x 194 cm. (79 x 78 in.).
Vicinity of Herculaneum.
Naples, Museo Archeologico
Nazionale.

Opposite

Doves

Mosaic in the Second Style.
113 x 113 cm. (44 x 44 in.).
House of the Mosaic Doves, Pompeii.

Editors: Jean-Claude Dubost and Jean-François Gonthier
English adaptation: Jean-Marie Clarke
Cover design: Gérard Lo Monaco and Laurent Gudin
Art Director: Hélène Lévi
Editing: Aude Simon and Malina Stachurska
Composition: Graffic, Paris
Filmsetting: Compo Rive Gauche, Paris
Lithography: Litho Service T. Zamboni, Verona

English edition, copyright © 1996
World copyright © 1995
by
FINEST S.A./EDITIONS PIERRE TERRAIL, PARIS
A subsidiary of the Book Department
of ⓢ Bayard Presse S.A.
ISBN: 2-87939-007-9
Printed in Italy

TABLE OF CONTENTS

Venus removing her sandal

Opus sectile (polychrome marble
inlay). 1st cent. A.D.
29 x 24 cm. (11 x 9 in.)
Triclinium in House I, 2, 10, Pompeii.
Naples, Museo Archeologico
Nazionale.

IN THE SHADOW OF A VOLCANO

Bacchus and Vesuvius

Fresco in the Fourth Style.
140 x 101 cm. (55 x 40 in.).
Peristyle of the House of the
Centenary, Pompeii.
Naples, Museo Archeologico
Nazionale.

Bacchus, together with his attributes –
a thyrsus (staff decorated with ivy
leaves) and a panther – is represented
in the form of a giant bunch of grapes.
Behind him stands Vesuvius, whose
vineyards were a major asset
in the Pompeian economy. In the
foreground winds a snake, symbolizing
the fertility of the soil.

On the morning of August 24th. 79 A.D., life seemed to roll on peacefully at the foot of Vesuvius. The region around the volcano was densely populated and fertile. The plains were dotted with towns, farms, smallholdings, and cultivated plots providing the cities with fresh produce, while the coast was lined with luxurious villas owned by the wealthy Roman aristocracy.

Nothing in particular hinted at impending disaster. As usual on a summer's day, the men and women of Pompeii had been busy since the early morning hours with their various occupations in town and in the fields. In thousands of homes, evening meals were already simmering on the hearth. In the bakers' ovens, large round loaves with rosette designs were baking to the desired golden brown, while in the neighbouring farms, amphoras and jars were being set aside to receive the wine from the new harvest.

From the square in front of the Temple of Venus, distant ships bearing precious cargoes from Egypt could be seen sailing on a light summer breeze towards the port at the mouth of the Sarno, the river which watered the lush valley at the foot of Vesuvius. Noontime had come and gone, and the intense summer heat forced people to leave their work and head for refreshment at the many *thermopolia*[1] (inexpensive eating houses) or to make their

1. See glossary.

way to the public baths for relaxation after the exertions of the day. Suddenly, a thundering roar caused everyone to look up towards the summit of Vesuvius, the volcano that rose majestically behind the colonnade of the forum and the Temple of Jupiter Capitoline, towering protectively over the peaceful landscape and in whose shadow the city snuggly nestled.

This time, however, the gaze of the Pompeians did not turn earthwards again to the vineyards that grew almost to the crater rim of the volcano and produced the famous *Vesuvinum*. There was something different about the ominous rumbling. The long dormant volcano – which one painter had depicted in the House of the Centenary alongside Bacchus personified as a giant bunch of grapes – had sprung to life again and was about to reveal its true nature as an exterminating force of nature.

THE FURY OF VESUVIUS

The mouth of the long inactive volcano suddenly spewed out a deadly column of gas and ash with unprecedented violence; this rose to twenty, then thirty thousand meters in the air, forming an anvil-shaped cloud that plunged the entire area into complete darkness. Formidable earth tremors shook the houses and caused the sea to recede from the coast. Within instants, the horrified Pompeians found themselves bombarded by a dense hail of *lapilli*[2] propelled by a violent windstorm. Ashes and cinders penetrated everywhere, filling every nook and cranny, accumulating on the roofs, which soon caved in under the sheer weight. In the space of twelve hours, the city was engulfed under a three-meter layer of volcanic debris.

During the night of the 25th, around one o'clock in the morning, the pressure of the volcanic gases suddenly eased and the eruption ceased. But over the next seven hours, waves of burning lava flowed down the slopes of Vesuvius and *surges* – clouds of fine cinders moving at speeds of from 60 to 250 meters per second (200-800 feet per second) – swept across the plain, burning all the vegetation and asphyxiating those trapped in its deadly stranglehold. The most destructive wave of lava which caused the greatest loss of human life came around six in the

1. See glossary.

morning. Finally, the eruption crater collapsed and added to the existing layer of lapilli a compact layer of cinerite or solidified ash between 50 and 150 centimeters (1.5 and 12 feet) thick. During the next few days, great quantities of pumice continued to fall, adding another 50 centimeters (1.5 foot) of debris to the covering layer. This was the final phase of the eruption. By then, a layer of volcanic material almost five meters thick had accumulated over the city and its vicinity.

The collapse of the volcanic cone released a flood of magma and lava which emerged from faults and flowed toward the neighbouring town of Herculaneum. Within hours, the town was buried under a layer of mud and detritus twelve meters thick, reaching twenty two meters near the seashore. This layer of material continued to spread, entirely covering the town, and eventually solidifed to the consistency of tuff. Ironically, it was precisely this suffocating layer which ultimately permitted the two cities to be preserved nearly intact for posterity.

View of the harbour
Fresco in the Fourth Style.
24 x 26 cm. (9 x 10 in.).
Naples, Museo Archeologico
Nazionale.

IMAGES OF DEATH

The Pompeians, overwhelmed and dismayed by this sudden explosion of natural forces, had reacted in different ways. At the first signs of the impending cataclysm, some instinctively sought shelter from the hail of rocks in their houses and cellars. Many died in this way, crushed in their own houses by the roofs collapsing under the weight of the lapilli or shaken by the tremors of the earthquake. Many skeletons were found lying on the ground in houses, crushed by the rubble, as in a recent case discovered in the house of Julius Polybius. Not long ago, a bakery (Reg. IX, 12, 6)[3] was excavated in which the corpses of the mules that turned the millstones were also found. The heavy beams supporting the roof had fallen on the backs of the unfortunate beasts who had managed to flee from the stables, but were trapped in the house hastily abandoned by owners who no doubt expected to return. In the famous house of Paquius Proculus, a little dog – whose presence was eerily prefigured by a mosaic in the entrance – was found rolled up into a ball under a

2. In the nineteenth century, archaeologists divided Pompeii into nine distinct sections, or regions. Each region consisted of several numbered *insulae*, or blocks. Houses and buildings in these blocks were also numbered. Thus, the reference IX, 12, 6 indicates a building – in this case a bakery – located at number 6 of block 12 in region IX.

bed in the corner usually slept in by the house guardian, or *atriensis*: the poor creature had instinctively sought refuge there, but on this occasion instinct had proved fatal.

The inhabitants of Herculaneum, which was struck only by the second phase of the eruption, had had more time to prepare their flight and thus had a greater chance of survival. But those who tried to flee seawards in boats and ships were repulsed by an awesome tidal wave that first emptied the bay of water before surging shorewards with terrible destructive force, cutting off access to the open sea. On the site of the ancient shoreline, an overturned boat was found along with the skeletons of people who had vainly sought shelter under some arches, trapped between the raging sea on the one side and the inexorably advancing mass of mud on the other.

Many Pompeians also tried to flee the city, some managing even to carry away their more precious belongings. They were among the lucky ones; a few hours walk put sufficient distance between them and Vesuvius or they found safety or adequate shelter on the nearby slopes of Mt. Lattari. Many more remained trapped in the city, however, wandering blindly through the labyrinthine streets on mounting layers of rocks and ash which soon rose all the way up to the roofs of the lower houses. They were joined during the apocalyptic night that followed by those who had survived the lapilli storm and unwisely returned to the city, thinking that the eruption had come to an end. For them, there was to be no escape: the shock wave of the surges with its incandescent clouds of toxic gases caught them totally unawares, suffocating them instantly.

Their bodies were covered with a layer of fine burning volcanic ash which clung to them like a glove, moulding every detail of their skin and clothing, even their facial expressions. When it cooled and hardened, the ash formed a compact mass around the bodies and soon, following the natural process of decomposition, only a hollow cavity in the solidified ash remained.

In the eighteenth century, the Bourbon king, who had organized the first official excavations in the region around Vesuvius, founded a museum at Portici on the outskirts of Naples. In one of the museum display-cases could be seen a piece of this solidified ash presenting the perfect mould of an

adolescent girl's breast. Madame de Staël was amazed and moved by the sight of this breast, and it was to inspire Théophile Gautier's short story, *Arria Marcella*.

The archaeologist Giuseppe Fiorelli, whose methods had a decisive scientific influence on the Pompeii excavations in the latter half of the nineteenth century, had the idea of injecting plaster into the cavities, the presence of which had been detected. As if by magic, there emerged the terrified faces of the victims of the eruption, the poignant sufferings of the little dog left attached to its chain, and the bodies of men, women and children desperately trying to escape from the inferno, struck down by death while vainly trying to protect their mouths with their hands.

At Opolontis, on the outskirts of Pompeii, a resin cast was recently made of a woman who was carrying her jewels and a bag containing coins, rings and precious stones. In the south-west section of the city, plaster casts of other victims of the eruption have recently been made: the most heartrending specimen is that of a man apparently trying to shield a pregnant woman with his own body. Several years ago, during the excavation of the *insula occidentalis*, a tragic scene was brought to light: a woman stretching out her arms to take the child which the father, on the point of dying, was holding out to her. Nothing, however, expressed more intensely the drama and poignancy of this catastrophe than the discovery of the mutilated bodies of little children caught in the throes of death.

PLINY'S ACCOUNT

Pliny the Younger, who witnessed the events which brought about the total destruction of one of the most famous sites in Campania, left a detailed and breathtaking account of the eruption and its aftermath in the form of two letters written to the historian Tacitus. The writer, then at Misenum staying with his uncle Pliny the Elder, commander of the Prætorian fleet in the Tyrrhenian Sea, anchored offshore, described in detail the various phases of the eruption, the panic of the inhabitants as they tried desperately to escape their cruel fate, and the death of his uncle. With the detached interest of a scientist, Pliny the Elder had dispatched his ships to observe the event from closer range, then, quickly realizing the gravity of the situation, had tried to rescue the inhabitants for whom escape by sea offered the sole hope of salvation. His efforts were all in vain. After an attempted landing at Herculaneum which had proved impossible because of the massive waves crashing against the shore, he then sought refuge in the nearby town of Stabiae, but fell victim to the clouds of toxic gas and perished.

When the blind fury of nature had abated, the entire balance of a region famed throughout the ancient world for its mild climate, varied landscapes, fertile fields and prosperous inhabitants had been profoundly disrupted. Whole towns had been engulfed, streets had vanished, and fields rendered barren. Those who had been fortunate enough to escape the catastrophe were left confronted by a spectacle of utter desolation.

FACE TO FACE WITH ANTIQUITY

Street in Pompeii

The streets of Pompeii were paved
with basalt flagstones and bordered
with high sidewalks. The streets
had no gutters and were impossible
to negotiate on rainy days. The large
basalt blocks in the middle allowed
pedestrians to cross the street without
wetting their feet or disturbing traffic.
The ruts visible on this photograph
were worn out by the passage of carts.
Some streets were paved as early
as the second century B.C., and
others covered with basalt flags during
the colonial period, or in any case
before Caesar's time. Other streets
remained unpaved.

A disaster of unprecedented magnitude had struck a region described by the ancients as *felix*, the "happy" land. News of the calamity quickly spread, inspiring shock and terror throughout the contemporary world. Martial, the Roman poet and a friend of Pliny the Younger, expressed people's horror in an emotion-filled dirge lamenting the tragic fate of Pompeii: "Here is Vesuvius, only yesterday covered still with greenery and shaded by vineyards from which the most savoury wines once flowed like rivers. Here is the mountain that Bacchus preferred even to the hills of Nyza, where Satyrs were wont to dance. Such was Pompeii, the city sacred to Venus, dearer to her heart than Sparta itself. And here was the proud town of Herculaneum, named in homage to the great hero. Yet now all lies wretchedly engulfed in flames and ashes. The gods themselves wish today that such a thing might have been beyond their power to perpetrate".

Herculaneum was totally submerged by mud already in the process of solidifying, and any attempt at salvage had become futile. In Pompeii, however, frantic efforts were underway to recover belongings from the houses, which could be entered via the roofs still protruding through the layer of volcanic dust and lapilli. The emperor Titus tried to restore a semblance of order by appointing *curatores* to protect the ruins from looters, and it

Via del Lupanare
Pompeii.

Opposite

Street with pedestrian passage
allowing safe crossing on rainy days.
Pompeii.

is no doubt thanks to these guards that many of the bronze and marble statues from the forum and public spaces were safely retrieved. But the salvage operations soon proved ineffective because of the high risks and costs involved. A deathly silence fell over the city and the surrounding countryside; for centuries afterwards, few human beings ventured to settle in the area devastated by the eruption.

In an uncanny anticipation of the sentiments later expressed by those who rediscovered the site, several years after the catastrophe which had wiped out cities and destroyed once fertile countryside, the poet Statius asked incredulously: "Will the next generation of men believe, when crops grow again and these desert fields are once more covered with flowers, that under their feet, whole cities and their populations lie buried, and that the fields of their forefathers sank into the abysmal depth?"

Indeed, after centuries of oblivion, when the excavation workers hired by Charles of Bourbon dug into the earth and came upon the city, with its portico-lined streets and squares, its houses and temples, shops and public buildings, all incredibly preserved thanks to the lapilli that had destroyed their occupants, they were awestruck by their prodigious discovery.

THE REDISCOVERY OF POMPEII

Goethe, the most famous of the eighteenth-century visitors to the site of the first systematic excavations conducted by the Bourbon administration, was indeed somewhat disappointed, but could immediately grasp the importance of this find and its priceless contribution to man's knowledge of Antiquity. For him, as for most of the educated men of his day, the notion of Antiquity was exclusively that which was portrayed in the memorable writings of Classical historians devoted to the Rome of the Cæsars, or inspired by the magnificent vestiges of the amphitheatres, imperial palaces, columns, and triumphal arches celebrating its glory. It was this shining heritage, full of noble rhetoric and images, that impressed and moved the minds of all who admired it.

Now, suddenly confronted with the piles of stonework bonded roughly together with mortar, the cramped dwellings, and the

Above

Thermopolium

Tavern. 1st cent. A.D.
Pompeii.

Pompeii had many *thermopolia*,
outdoor stands where drinks (mostly
wine diluted with water) were sold; at
least 89 have been found. Customers
could also buy a snack between meals.
The stone counters decorated
with pieces of marble still have
the earthenware jars in which the food
and wine were stored.

Opposite

**Doorway seen
from a thermopolium**

1st cent. A.D.
Herculaneum.

Streetside fountain
Limestone. 1st cent. A.D.
Pompeii.

Street
Herculaneum.

The **"Arch of Tiberius"**
1st cent. A.D.
Via di Mercurio, Pompeii.

banal everyday objects, the great poet had difficulty in connecting such mundane realities to the Roman grandeur that had so often inspired his dreams. In the diary he kept during his Italian journey, in the entry dated March 11th. 1787, Goethe wrote of "doll's houses" and "little papier-maché models." These commonplace vestiges were utterly devoid of the great classical and universal spirit of Antiquity which had nourished his ideals. Nevertheless, a man of Goethe's genius could not fail to grasp the entirely new perspectives that were thus opened up to human knowledge. Here it was the spirit of real people, as they had actually lived at the time, which infused the stones of the buildings, the meeting places, and the walls of the houses with a tangible and material presence. Two days later, expressing the very essence of the fate which had befallen the Vesuvian city, the poet noted in his journal these laconic, ostensibly cynical lines: "Of all the catastrophes which have been visited upon the world, few have bequeathed such enormous benefit to future generations."

As excavation works progressed and extended in scope, it was plain that no mere isolated monument, tomb or ruin was being disinterred; what was coming to light was an entire urban fabric suddenly stopped in its tracks, frozen in time, unveiled in all its complexity to modern eyes. What was being unearthed was Antiquity itself, revealing in the slightest detail, and in its most intimate and secret aspects, all the nuances and multiple facets of a former way of life. Emerging from under the rubble were the tastes, manners and customs of a long vanished society.

Above

Forum

Detail.
1st cent. A.D.
Pompeii.

This photograph shows the pedestals
on which statues of famous citizens
were mounted.

Opposite

Scene in the forum

Fresco. Mid-1st cent. A.D.
64 x 48 cm. (25 x 19 in.).
House of Juius Felix, Pompeii.
Naples, Museo Archeologico
Nazionale.

This painting depicts equestrian
statues standing near the porticoes of
the forum.

THE BIRTH
OF A CITY

Apollo

Bronze. 1st cent. A.D.
Temple of Apollo, Pompeii.
The original is in the Naples Museum.

Although the statue reiterates certain
Grecian stylistic features,
the technique is typically Italic
in its harmonious treatment
of volumes and unaffected liveliness
of movement.

When the eruption of Vesuvius in 79 A.D. put an effective end to the city's existence, Pompeii already had a long history behind it, stretching back to the late seventh century B.C.

The site chosen for the foundation of the city was a low hill formed by an eruption of the volcano in prehistoric times. It overlooked the delta in which the Sarno River, on its passage to the sea, widened out into a kind of lagoon offering an ideal harbour for ships of heavy tonnage. The site, however, had numerous disadvantages, in particular regarding the supply of fresh water for which deep wells had to be sunk. The possibility that Pompeii grew "naturally", the result of the spontaneous accumulation of dwellings and facilities at a nexus of intensive communication, can be dismissed. It would be mistaken to think that such a place, located fairly high up on the edge of a vast plain, might have stood at the crossroads of major routes; these, rather than going through Pompeii, could more easily have skirted round it. The main advantage of the site was its strategic hill-top position which permitted easy supervision of traffic at the mouth of the Sarno River and along the entire coast.

THE OPICS

Archaeological excavations in the Sarno valley have brought to light many burial places and settlements from both prehistoric and earliest recorded times. All are located in the vicinity of the river, like the Bronze Age village recently discovered near the mouth of the Sarno, in an area called San Abbandio, part of present-day Pompeii. The village of Sarno itself was located near a spring, and other villages in the valley – Striano, San Marzano, San Valentino Torio – were settled between the ninth and sixth centuries B.C.

The Opic populations that lived in the valley at the end of the prehistoric age were essentially agricultural. They seem to have had a sedentary way of life at first, and were organized into loosely hierarchized communities. Later, although they continued to live in numerous small settlements each disposing of a large stretch of land along the valley, the social structure began to stratify into distinct classes as a result of outside influences, in particular the cultural and commercial exchanges which developed with the Greek colony founded at Cumae around the middle of the eighth century B.C. As the funerary treasures found in tombs from this period attest, the rich made a conspicuous display of their wealth and social status.

This state of affairs was suddenly changed by the emergence of an entirely new, and indeed revolutionary, factor: the foundation of the city.

ETRUSCANS, GREEKS AND THE FOUNDATION OF THE CITY

The choice of a relatively high and steep site overlooking the sea for the foundation of Pompeii must have been made for purely strategic reasons: to control and protect the coastal parts of the mouth of the Sarno, the main access route into the fertile valley. For a long time, Pompeii was protected by walls that encircled the entire hillside; dwellings were still sparse, being restricted to the area around the forum and the terrace that extended it to the south-east.

The foundation of the city was probably linked to the spread of the Etruscan civilization in southern Campania. Thanks to

Above

Tuff columns
Late 2nd cent. B.C.
Forum, Pompeii.

On the south-east side of the forum stand columns made of grey tuff from Nocera; these originally belonged to the first portico built by the quaestor Vibrius Popidius at the end of the Samnite Period.

Opposite

Columns in the forum
Detail.

their possession of raw materials such as iron, much in demand at
the time, the future founders of Rome had seen their economic
power grow and, through their trade relations with the Greek
world, Etruscan culture had blossomed. At this stage, however,
they must have felt that the powerful and prosperous colonies
which the Greeks had established along the Campanian coast
and elsewhere to protect their own trade routes constituted an
obstacle to Etruscan expansion in Southern Italy.

Etruscan civilization was essentially urban. There is evidence
suggesting that they joined forces with the local population to
create fortified centres – clearly a move to consolidate their
strategic interests. This hypothesis is supported by the fact that,
at about the same time, two cities were founded in the Sarno
plain: Pompeii, which was intended to control river and coastal
traffic, and Nocera – located at the extreme opposite end of the
valley, in the narrow gorge separating the foothills of the
Apennines from the Lattari mountains – which was intended to
control the overland routes between southern Campania and
the South. Subsequently, the respective histories of these two
cities were to be closely linked.

During this early phase, two sanctuaries – always very strong
poles of cultural attraction in Antiquity – were built in Pompeii.
The first was dedicated to the cult of Apollo and located near the
open space which served as marketplace and place of assembly in
the centre of the city and which later became the forum. The
second was a Doric temple built on the south terrace, directly
overlooking the sea. Set on a rocky promontory, it was easily
visible from the open sea and so formed an important landmark
for shipping. Features such as the dedicatory inscription of the
Temple of Apollo and the Doric columns of the second temple
reveal the decisive influence of Greek culture upon the Etruscans.
Stratigraphic surveys inside the Temple of Apollo have brought to
light many objects of Greek importation, as well as typically
Etruscan black ceramic, or *bucchero*, vases. Other objects also bore
inscriptions in Etruscan, proof of the active presence of this
culture in the city, as well as in the Sorrento peninsula and in the
Sarno Valley, as far as Nocera. The complexity of the social and
ethnic fabric in southern Campania is demonstrated by the
discovery at Nocera and Vico Equense of two inscriptions written
in a local alphabet – traces of which have also been found in

central Italy. These inscriptions have provided invaluable information about the Italic populations of the Sarno Valley, traditionally referred to as the Opics in the earliest historical texts.

THE ARRIVAL OF THE SAMNITES

After the final collapse of Etruscan power, brought about by a coalition of Greek cities after the second Battle of Cumae in 474 B.C., followed by the massive incursion of Samnite tribes from the Apennines in the late fifth century B.C., the region around Pompeii underwent profound transformations.

The Greek colonists now fully controlled Campania and were confident of having eliminated their Etruscan rivals once and for all. The Samnites seized the territories which the coastally based Greeks had either not wished to, or not been in a position to occupy on a permanent basis. Pompeii thus became an Oscan city, part of a Samnite confederation which included Herculaneum, Sorrento and Stabiae, with its capital in Nocera.

The foundation of Herculaneum probably dates from the Samnite Period. It was originally a small citadel, set on a rocky promontory overlooking the sea, lying between two rivers that flowed at the foot of Vesuvius. Archaeological excavations up till now have yielded no objects or traces prior to the fourth century B.C., although ancient texts claim a far older origin. Hercules was said to have been the eponymous founder of the city which was successively occupied by the Opics, the Etruscans and then the Samnites. Excavations in the city so far, however, have involved only a small portion of the inhabited zone covering barely a dozen acres.

Pompeii began to expand during the Samnite Period. Blocks of houses, virtually square in design, were built to the east of the Via Strabiana. In the future Roman city, this street would be extended toward the Porta Vesuvio to become the main North-South axis, or *cardo*. The city continued to spread, especially to the north, in the zone today included in Region VI, which, although a focus of great activity, remained outside the city center in the earliest period. Samnite dignitaries built their residential quarter there, overlooking the Via di Mercurio to the north of the Via del Foro. Their houses were grouped into long

Above and opposite

Architrave fragments from a portico

1st cent. B.C.
Forum, Pompeii.

The architrave of the portico, replaced with travertine under Augustus, held a second row of columns as well as the floor of a raised ambulatory which commanded a view of the forum.

rectangular blocks which stood, with little major alteration to their original structure or outward appearance over the course of the centuries, until the destruction of the city in 79 A.D.

The original ramparts had been built with volcanic stone that had the consistency of tuff; when these were replaced by stronger fortifications, granitic limestone, quarried in the foothills of the Apennines near the source of the Sarno, was used. These new defences were in turn reinforced, probably in the wake of Hannibal's military campaign at the end of the third century B.C. Finally, one century later, they were embellished by the provision of a series of well-aligned whitewashed towers built at regular intervals. Standing like sentinels guarding the plain below, these towers symbolized the city's power.

HANNIBAL IN CAMPANIA

During the Second Punic War, the entire Sarno Valley suffered the ravages perpetrated by looting and raiding armies led by Hannibal, one of the greatest military commanders of Antiquity. Nocera, capital of the Oscan confederation of southern Campania, had become a faithful ally of Rome after the Samnite wars, and was besieged and sacked by the Carthaginians. Many of the surviving inhabitants were taken in by surrounding towns, especially Atella, where most of the Nocerans took refuge until their city could be rebuilt.

After the Punic War, Pompeii again expanded, this time towards the east. New blocks of rectangular dwellings were built along the two main *decumani*, or east-west axes, from the Via di Nola in the north, and the Via dell'Abbondanza in the south, stretching beyond the old street alignment and extending the inhabited area to the eastern fortifications. The volcanic hill, which, from earliest times, the foresighted ancients had prudently ringed with ramparts, was almost entirely covered with buildings.

Recent stratigraphic surveys in this area have shown that a series of rather small identical houses were built in a checkerboard pattern, each provided with an inner courtyard and a vegetable garden in the back. In the following period, the need for housing having diminished with the reconstruction of Nocera, these small houses were demolished and the land turned

Portico in the triangular forum

2nd cent. B.C.
Pompeii.

This portico is one of the vestiges of the triangular forum, one of the oldest public places in the city (built during the second half of the Second century B.C.). The triangular forum was designed as part of a precise urban scheme and is architecturally and ideologically related to the theatre district.

over to agriculture; vineyards and flower gardens were planted to produce the floral essences used in the manufacture of perfumes.

THE LUXURY OF THE SECOND SAMNITE PERIOD

Towards the end of the Samnite Period, during the closing decades of the second century B.C., Pompeii experienced one of the most flourishing periods of its history. The new markets in the Mediterranean basin, especially in the East, which the Romans had opened up to their Italic allies, brought increased prosperity to a society whose ruling class already enjoyed the advantage of a solid economic and productive structure based on vast agricultural estates, the *latifundia*. Signs of the wealth accumulated by merchants from their profitable maritime trading activity were in ample evidence throughout the city.

Towards the end of the century, an ambitious renovation programme was undertaken in Pompeii: the central square or forum was enhanced with a monumental portico composed of two superimposed rows of columns. This portico featured two orders – Doric on the first level and Ionic on the second – linking between them elements from a variety of periods and styles. The Temple of Jupiter, the largest religious building in the city, stood majestically on the longitudinal axis of the forum closing the perspective to the north. Towards the end of the second century B.C., a fish-and meat-market, or *macellum*, was built to the east of the temple; this was followed by a *basilica*, the main municipal building where justice was administered, the centre of public life where people met to conduct business or to keep abreast of the latest news.

Another important public works project was carried out at this period near the Doric temple. It featured a monumental entrance and propylaea with Ionic columns on the side facing the centre of the city. This irregular, roughly triangular-shaped space was given precise geometric form by a triple portico which extended southwards, opening out onto the terrace and a vast perspective of the sea backed by the Lattari mountains.

This central space, which already housed a gymnnasium, was then astutely linked via the rocky south-west promontory to the flank of the hill where terraced seats had been hewn out for a vast open-air theatre. The Doric temple thus enclosed the theatre

esplanade, serving as a shrine for the worship of the gods to whom the performances (originally sacred mystery plays) were dedicated, and forming part of an architectural project with a distinctly Hellenistic flavour. The ensemble was completed by a large portico behind the stage which was used as a foyer during intermissions or between performances and also served a small adjacent covered theatre designed for lyrical performances – poetic recitals accompanied by lyre music.

This ambitious architectural project, however, was not completed during the Samnite Period. Events were coming to a head and the Italic populations were threatening rebellion against Rome. Unlike the wars waged in previous centuries, it was no longer a matter of asserting Samnite supremacy – even less independence from a power which had conquered much of the known world – but rather of obtaining the much-coveted right of Roman citizenship, with all the economic and legal advantages that this entailed.

ROMAN COLONIZATION

During the ensuing civil war, which lasted from 90 until 88 B.C., the Italic allies fought against the army led by the Roman general Lucius Cornelius Sulla and Pompeii was besieged. When the fateful eruption occurred one hundred and seventy years later, traces of these dramatic events were still visible in the city: on certain street corners can be seen inscriptions in Oscan giving directions to the hastily-assembled confederate reinforcements to where best to deploy along the ramparts in order to repel the enemy assault. All, however, was in vain. Crushed by Roman military superiority, Pompeii was defeated and forced to capitulate. Shortly after, Herculaneum suffered a similar fate.

Conquered by Sulla's troops, Herculaneum became a *municipium*, and in 80 B.C. Pompeii was proclaimed a colony subject to Roman law. From then on, like the other townships in the region, Pompeii became closely dependent on the political, administrative, social and economic policies adopted by its new masters. The latter stripped the old Oscan aristocrats of their powers and expropriated their estates, building luxurious villas and soon transforming Pompeii, like so many other cities of Campania, into a fashionable vacation resort for wealthy Romans.

Above

Altar
Marble. 1st cent. A.D.
Temple of Vespasian, Pompeii.

Opposite

Animal sacrifice
Detail.
Marble bas-relief. 1st cent. A.D.
Altar from the Temple of Vespasian, Pompeii.

The altar, which survived the looting after the eruption, depicts a sacrificial scene on the side facing the forum. The officiant and his assistant lead the bull about to be sacrificed, while a priest, his head covered, pours a libation on a tripod. In the background we can see a flutist, lictors with the magistrate's insignia of office, and servants holding accessories for the ritual.

The odeum

Cavea and proedria.
First half of the 1st cent. B.C.
Pompeii.

The Small Theatre, which was
covered, had a seating capacity of
1,500 and was used for lyrical
performances: i.e. poetry recitals
accompanied by lyre music. At the
ends of the balustrade separating
the caeva from the *proedria* – which
had wider seats for the city notables –
can be seen winged lions, carved in
tuff. Higher up is a *telamon* figure, also
in tuff.

The healthy climate and incomparably beautiful landscape were ideally suited to the leisurely life of the masters, while the exceptionally fertile lands and the availability of cheap slave labour guaranteed high crop yields and substantial land and property revenues. The names of many Roman aristocrats who held estates in and around Pompeii have come down to us. The most famous among them during the Republican Period was the great orator and politician Marcus Tullius Cicero (106-43 B.C.), who has left many letters written from his beloved *Pompeianum*.

The architecture of this period, naturally, complied with the canons of the new regime. The Samnite magistrates having been expelled, their splendid houses passed into the hands of Roman colonists, who proceeded to redesign and convert them. The Temple of Jupiter became the Capitol, the tangible symbol of Roman power over the colonized formerly-independent city; the old *thermae* at Stabiae were restored, while new bathing facilities were built near the forum. A temple dedicated to Venus, Sulla's tutelary deity, was built near the basilica on a special raised terrace so as to provide a landmark like the Doric temple. The cult of Venus was adroitly associated with that of the local fertility goddess, and the city was rebaptized *Colonia Cornelia Veneria Pompeianorum*, or the city of the "cult of Venus Pompeiana."

The splendid villa of Diomedes was ruthlessly carved in two in order to lay out a new axis leading to the northwest gate of the city. The construction programme in the theatre district culminated with the building of a great covered hall, while a twenty-thousand seat amphitheatre was built at the far south-east perimeter. Construction of this amphitheatre, the oldest one that has come down to us, was probably already underway during the Samnite Period.

THE NEW AUGUSTAN ERA

During the reign of Augustus (27 B.C.-14 A.D.), and with the advent of the Imperial Period, the architecture became more formal and propaganda-oriented. Augustus, who had the delicate task of leading Rome towards a type of government better adapted to its status as world power, required full support and approval from his subjects. His first task was to consolidate the power which he had progressively acquired, but which he

The odeum
First half of the 1st cent. B.C.
Pompeii.

Telamon

Tuff sculpture. First half of the
1st cent. B.C. Odeum, Pompeii.

The tuff telamons in the odeum are
significant examples of the sculptural
tradition transmitted by the
Hellenistic culture, which was still
vibrant at the beginning of the Roman
colonization.

could only exercise by usurping and monopolizing a series of constitutional institutions for which an illusory republican guise was preserved by astute legal manoeuvering. In order to effect a smooth transition from republic to empire, he was forced to generate a broad consensus and to seek the backing and cooperation of the municipal administrations in the peninsula.

This new political line naturally required the support of the wealthy local middle classes. The case of Pompeii is particularly instructive in this respect, all the more so in that Augustus' reforms had attached Campania to Latium in order to create the first administrative district. Thus, during the first Imperial Period, representatives of the indigenous families, which had formed the backbone of the social edifice before being ousted by Sulla, were gradually re-admitted into the power structure at the highest echelons. Augustus granted them special privileges, promoting some of them to the knighthood or offering other perquisites. He looked on benevolently as they resumed the prominent role in local affairs which had been the prerogative of their forefathers. In return, whole sections of the population devoted themselves to the cult of the emperor which was officiated by the *Augustales*, or the priests of Augustus, rich freemen who had been granted an official role commensurate with their economic power and entrepreneurial talent – the magistrature remaining closed to them because of their non-Roman birth. These officials took charge of public works, occasionally supplementing state subsidies for the erection of grand public buildings with a personal financial contribution and thus bolstering imperial propaganda.

Social harmony having been re-established, the new political order felt the need to make its mark through a building programme intended to concretely demonstrate the well-being and prosperity which the new "golden age" was bringing to the Roman world. The city was decked out in marble and adorned with statuary. In the forum, new colonnades made of travertine – a decorative white limestone resembling marble – were erected, while the old tuff columns were replaced with this nobler material. The old pavement was replaced with travertine flagstones featuring laudatory inscriptions picked out in bronze letters. The main buildings in the city were restored, enlarged and embellished. The wine growers and exporters added an upper gallery with a

Theatre mask
Detail.
Fresco in the Second Style.
118 x 60 cm. (46 x 24 in.).
Region VI, *insula occidentalis*, 4,
Pompeii.
Naples, Museo Archeologico
Nazionale.

Fighting in the amphitheatre

Fresco painted between 59 and 79 A.D.
169 x 185 cm. (67 x 73 in.).
House I, 3, 23, Pompeii.
Naples, Museo Archeologico
Nazionale.

twin external arcade to the large theatre and dedicated it to Augustus. A certain Tullius had a temple dedicated to Fortuna Augusta built on a plot of land belonging to him. To promote the paramilitary-style sporting activities which Augustus actively encouraged, a new gymnasium with a large central swimming pool was built near the amphitheatre. In Herculaneum, another wealthy citizen named M. Nonius Balbus commissioned the building of a basilica and supervised the restoration of the ramparts. A truly colossal project involving a new aqueduct was undertaken to channel fresh water down from the mountains to the fleet anchored off Misenum in the Gulf of Naples, and to at long last provide Herculaneum and Pompeii with a supply of running water, not only for the public fountains and baths, but also for private homes. The gardens were embellished with ornamental water basins, statues and niches decorated with polychrome glass mosaics, and even monumental *nympahea*, or artifical grottoes, where the rich and their guests could while away the hot afternoon hours to the gentle murmur of the fountains.

AUGUSTUS' SUCCESSORS

The emperors who succeeded Augustus, Tiberius in particular, continued this policy of imperial propaganda of which architecture, today, provides the the most tangible legacy. One of the most typical examples is the edifice which the priestess Eumachia commissioned on the forum for the fullers' guild; in fact, it was also used by the woolmakers, dyers, and launderers, as well as for various commercial activities. Its impressive vestibule was decorated with statues and dedicatory inscriptions glorifying the illustrious ancestors of the Julia *gens* to which the imperial dynasty belonged. The triumphal arch raised to the east of the Temple of Jupiter closed the forum on the north side. Its niches probably housed statues of members of the imperial family, while the monument was crowned by an equestrian statue. The triumphal arch standing farther north on the same road, at the beginning of the majestic prospect of the Via di Mercurio, was probably dedicated to Emperor Tiberius.

Over a period of several decades, life in Pompeii was peaceful and prosperous. In 59 B.C., however, serious conflicts broke out between the inhabitants of Pompeii and those of Nocera; violent

fighting in the amphitheatre was brutally repressed by the central authorities, who feared a popular uprising. The quarrel with Nocera concerned the territories which Nero had granted to this city when he had proclaimed it a Roman colony.

THE EARTHQUAKES
PRIOR TO THE ERUPTION

The most important event to upset the tranquility of Pompeii was the earthquake of February 5th. 62 A.D. Despite the extent of the cataclysm, the inhabitants summoned up the strength to react and to undertake an impressive reconstruction campaign involving both public and private buildings. For many years, the city was one vast construction site. In an extraordinary feat of energy, the Pompeians undertook new projects, such as the grandiose central baths which occupied an entire city block at the intersection of the Via Stabiana and the Via di Nola, or the temple of the *Lares Publici*, which was perhaps erected in the forum to exorcise the *prodigium* which had dealt the city such a fatal blow.

To be sure, the imperial administration – beginning with Nero, who with his wife Poppaea (a native of Pompeii)is often glorified in inscriptions, and followed by Vespasian, who had a temple in the forum dedicated to his own cult – supported the Pompeians' reconstruction effort. Despite these earnest efforts at rebuilding, the work was never to be completed. New tremors shook the city a short time before the fateful eruption of Vesuvius. The latest research shows that it was because of this later earthquake, and not that of 62 A.D., that public buildings were discovered in an unused state, along with houses still undergoing restoration work.

On August 24th. 79 A.D., when the final eruption put an end to its centuries-long existence, the city was still actively engaged in the process of healing the wounds caused by previous disasters. Vesuvius, the mighty mountain which until then had seemed so protective, had become the gateway through which the forces of nature were unmercifully unleashed on Pompeii, sealing its fate for all time.

Calidarium
1st cent. B.C.
Forum baths, Pompeii.

At the north end of the room used for hot baths there was a marble basin into which hot water was poured. Steam was dispersed by clay pipes between the ground and raised stone floor and upwards via interstices between the walls and the wall-cladding so that the entire room became one great radiator.
The barrel vault was lined with stucco fluting to channel the steam. In the foreground is a marble pool or *labrum* with cold-water fountains for instant refreshment. The bronze inscription that runs along the border commemorates the magistrates who had the facilities built and financed with public funds: 5,250 sesterces, a considerable amount at the time (a loaf of bread cost only half a sesterce).

Below

Basin in the calidarium
Detail.

IN SEARCH
OF AN IDENTITY

**Alexander and Darius
at the Battle of Issos**

Detail showing King Darius.
Mosaic in the First Style.
House of the Faun, Pompeii.
Naples, Museo Archeologico
Nazionale.

The vestiges from the earliest stages of the city's existence do not give a very precise picture of its social development. The rare evidence garnered from excavations has enabled us to sketch out only the roughest outline of cultural life. Not until the second Samnite Period, starting in the third century B.C., do we possess sufficient elements permitting us to determine the structure, layout and decoration of certain dwellings.

Before turning to this period, however, it is necessary to say something further about the Oscans, the early population of Pompeii, and more generally about the Italic populations of Samnite origin, to whom the Oscans themselves belonged and who have been unfairly neglected by historians.

CULTURE AND TASTES DURING THE SAMNITE PERIOD

The Italics, who developed a completely novel political ideal – that of federalism – had the misfortune of rebelling against Rome at a crucial time in their history – and losing. The triumphal Roman victory at the Battle of Sentinus in 29 B.C. relegated the Oscans to historical oblivion. And since history is written by the victors, the historians of Antiquity, naturally prejudiced in favour of Rome, have not painted a very flattering portrait of the Samnites, presenting them as uncouth highland

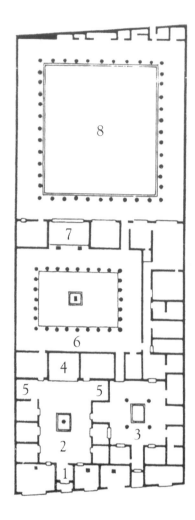

Plan of the House of the Faun

1. Vestibule
2. Main atrium
3. Tetrastyle atrium
4. Tablinum
5. Wing
6. First peristyle
7. Exedra
8. Second peristyle

Below

**Reconstitution of the atrium decor
in the House of the Faun**

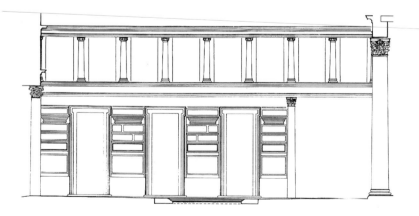

warriors with a basically primitive, tribal way of life. Not a single line of their writings, not a single text, has ever come down to us in translation, as if we were in the presence of a totally un-cultivated people. This was undoubtedly one consequence of the fatal attraction Rome exercised over conquered cultures.

Indirectly, a glimpse may be caught of the true intellectual wealth of Italic society in the middle of the fourth century B.C. by reading Cicero's account of the noble discussions between Archita, a Pythagorean philosopher and noted mathematician, and Gaius Pontius Samnita, a representative of the Samnite aristocracy. These conversations on the advantages of old age took place in Tarentum in the presence of Plato, a good friend of Archita's. It is quite unthinkable – and here we base our conjecture on probability rather than verifiable fact – that either Archita or Plato would have indulged in discussions of lofty philosophical import with an illiterate man who had not fully assimilated the cultural values of the Greek world. In all likelihood, the Samnite aristocracy to which Gaius Pontius belonged was more at home with such abstract considerations than with those pertaining to the mundane realities of everyday life.

Archeology has uncovered definite proof of the close involvement of the Italics with the Hellenic cultural world. The funerary treasures, painted tombs, and artistic vestiges tell of a society that was highly organized, both from the civil and military points of view, extensively Hellenized, and that enjoyed a much more refined lifestyle than even the Romans themselves.

HOUSES WITH AN ATRIUM

The urban layout, civic design, and public buildings of Pompeii are eloquent testimony to the way of thinking of its Samnite inhabitants, strongly influenced by Greek cultural models. The city has preserved splendid houses attesting to Samnite opulence and providing valuable and detailed information about its own architectural structure.

Despite later alterations, in dwellings such as the so-called House of the Surgeon (VI, 1, 10)[1] and the House of Sallustus (VI,

---

1. The names given to Pompeian houses in modern times rarely refer to their original owners, who are mostly unknown; more often than not they allude to some discovery made on the premises.

Tetrastyle atrium

2nd cent. B.C.
House of the Silver Wedding, Pompeii.

Pavement

Travertine, slate and green limestone.
First Style.
2nd cent. B.C.
Tablinum of the House of the Faun,
Pompeii.

The rich pavement decoration in the
room where *clientes* were received
presents patterns of light and dark
lozenges creating the illusion of cubes
in perspective. Because this type of
decor was often used in temple
sanctuaries, it endowed the room –
where the magistrate received visitors
seated on an impressive chair – with
a certain dignity and sacred character.

2, 4), it is still possible to recognize the original layout of the third century B.C. Italic houses of members of the property-owning class. These featured austere façades built in cubic blocks of tuff or limestone; the entrance was preceded by a vestibule which divided the space into two lateral rooms occasionally opening out onto the street and thus serving as small shops run by members of the household. The vestibule led directly to the *atrium*, an inner court in the centre of the house which gave access to various living rooms and bedrooms. The atrium was the heart of domestic life. In the middle of it stood an *impluvium*, a shallow pool which collected rainwater and channelled it to an underground cistern for everyday needs. The rain fell in through the *compluvium*, a roof-opening which also provided light for the inner rooms. These rarely had windows to the outside – at most a narrow champfered slit to admit more light. On the opposite side of the atrium from the vestibule was the *tablinum*, formerly the room where the master of the house stored the *tabulae*, or family archives and documents, but later serving as an office where he received his *clientes* – persons who, in some respect or other, were under his obligation and came to offer their services or solicit his help and protection. On either side of the tablinum ran two *alae*, or wings, which had no doors but gave directly onto the atrium; originally used to house the religious or ancestral idols worshipped by the family, these rooms later served for social functions, the reception of guests, etc. Behind the tablinum, a small kitchen garden provided fresh vegetables for everyday consumption.

THE CONCENTRATED DWELLING

It would be mistaken, however, to regard this type of house with atrium as the commonest type of dwelling. Recent stratigraphic samplings in the south-west part of the city, along the Via di Nocera, have lent support to a theory advanced by Hoffmann, an eminent Pompeii specialist. The study of some closely-built houses located in lot 11 of Region I has shown that, as early as the end of the third century B.C. or, at latest, the beginning of the second century B.C., there existed a completely different type of house from the one featuring an atrium.

These dwellings were built in uniform rows along the street-front; they were fairly small, less than 10 meters (33 feet) wide

Dancing Faun

Bronze.
Original from the 2nd cent. B.C.
Height 71 cm. (28 in.).
House of the Faun, Pompeii.
Naples, Museo Archeologico
Nazionale.

and with an indoor floor area of 120 sq meters (1,290 sq feet). A hallway about 3 meters (10 feet) long divided the space into two lateral rooms and led, not to an atrium, but to a central room disposed transversally and measuring less than 10 meters (33 feet) wide, and at most 5.5 meters (18 feet) long. This living room was the effective hub of domestic life and the link to the other parts of the house – additional 4-5 meter-long (13-16 feet-long) rooms located farther back – all connected by a corridor which led to a small backyard, probably a decorative garden, or *hortus*.

Recent studies have permitted the identification of other types of fairly similar houses. These dwellings belonged to members of a fairly homogeneous middle class who, although playing no important role in the social hierarchy, were sufficiently well-off to possess a small property catering for the family needs. The houses are all fairly unpretentious both as regards the building materials employed and the low-cost, rapid, and simple construction techniques involved. These dwellings were built in a peripheral zone of urban development, often in series of blocks, probably to provide accommodation for the many families that had fled the neighbouring towns in the wake of Hannibal's campaign and the destruction of Nocera. In a subsequent phase of construction, an upper story was added to these houses, all of which moreover, regardless of floor area, typically possessed a garden in the back.

Such gardens were an indispensable annex to the living space. Not only did they play a precise role in the domestic economy; in addition, they provide a revealing insight into the lifestyle and behaviour patterns of Pompeian society as a whole.

THE ATRIUM:
A PRESTIGIOUS SHOWCASE

The evolution of residential architecture among the privileged classes illustrates the growing opulence of a city which had built up extensive commercial and cultural relations with the Hellenistic world and was now in a position to project a prestigious image of itself. The elite, whose wealth had increased considerably during the second century B.C., wholeheartedly embraced the example of the dominant Roman culture, and soon began to rival it in magnificence.

While public architecture, with its colonnades, porticoes and grandiose buildings, displayed an obvious taste for the monumental, influential Pompeians strove to endow their own private sphere with a certain official stamp reflecting both their role in public life and their social status. Society was firmly in the hands of a small number of families who, fully conscious of their own importance and function, built sumptuous residences,

Frieze with masks
Mosaic in the First Style.
49 x 280 cm. (19 x 110 in.).
House of the Faun, Pompeii.
Naples, Museo Archeologico
Nazionale.

Frieze with masks
Details.

often on a par with royal palaces, to express their power and dominant rank. Although the structure of the dwelling altered, the original inspiration remained the same. The traditional floor-plan was retained, but expanded – new functions were added and new rooms were laid out. Certain features such as columns and colonnades, normally associated with public architecture, became an indispensable part of the decor.

Many examples of houses with double atriums have been found, especially in Region VI, the main residential quarter at the time: these include the House of the Faun (VI, 12, 2-5), the House of the Labyrinth (VI, 11, 9-10), the Houses of the Large (VI, 8, 20-22) and Small (VI, 8, 23-24) Fountains, the House of the Silverware (VI, 7, 20-21), and the House of the Centenary (IX, 8, 6). These two juxtaposed atriums had different functions. One was reserved exclusively for family use and was linked to the servants' quarters. The other atrium was used, as the case may be, as an open-air office where merchants received their clientèle, or as a private courtroom where magistrates dealt with political, judicial and other public matters. It was, in the words of the famous Roman architect Vitruvius, a place where the common people could go freely without waiting to be summoned. Certain rooms in the house were designed specifically for this purpose, and featured an architecture and decor which emphasized the respectability of the worthy proprietor receiving his clients and fellow citizens.

The houses built around a single atrium were themselves also designed to enhance the social and personal prestige of their owners in the eyes of visitors. The space was expanded, and four high columns crowned with magnificent capitals were erected around the impluvium, like those in the House of the Silver Wedding (V, 2, i), which support the rafters of the roof and compluvium, creating a distinctly theatrical effect and giving the house the sumptuous appearance of a Hellenistic palace. This is also the case with the "Corinthian" atrium in the House of the Dioscuri (VI, 9, 6) which has no less than twelve columns supporting the roof pitch, or with the House of the Diadumeni (IX, 1, 20), which has a total of sixteen.

Also to be found are vast atriums, built in an austere traditional Italic vein on the Tuscan model and featuring wooden beams rather than columns as load-bearing structural

elements; these likewise proclaimed the wealth of the proprietor. The difficulty of procuring beams of sufficient diameter and length to support a large roof, the technical skills involved, and the highly specialized workers required by such an installation made the construction of this type of atrium a very complex and costly affair, beyond the means of most Pompeian worthies. The latter usually opted for the much less expensive yet discreetly elegant solution of a simple patio with four columns. Whichever type of design was chosen, they all attest to the lavish care taken to create a majestic noble effect underlining the owners' social status. Family prestige was conspicuously displayed not only by such an integral feature of outward representation as rich decoration, but also by the architecture itself, as in the case of the atrium in the House of the Faun – a perfectly convincing reconstruction shows that this had a raised upper floor with a row of columns creating a sort of loggia.

HOUSES IN THE GREEK STYLE

The Hellenistic architecture of the Pompeian house underwent major changes during this period. More space was provided, and the vegetable garden located behind the tablinum was replaced by a garden surrounded by columns forming shaded porticoes – the

peristyle. The extensive use of columns, typical of both Greek civil and religious architecture, highlighted the interior volumes, as in the Greek *gymnasium*, and conferred a certain splendour to the whole. With its monumental columns, the peristyle, located at the heart of the private space, became the centre of social life in the home. Around the porticoes, different types of public and private rooms were disposed, all inspired by Greek models: *oeci, exedrae, diactae, triclinii, bibliothecae*, etc.[2]

The magistrate, who conducted his business and received his *clientes* in the atrium, hosted his friends in the peristyle, whiling away the hours in long conversation and congenial dinners, while torches and candelabras kept the darkness at bay. With their high windowless walls, the private houses were cut off from the outside world, and the gardens, with their roses and other fragrant plants – a pleasant change from the pungent smell of cabbage and turnips in the old vegetable gardens – now brought a much-needed touch of nature to the city. The very emblem of *luxuria*, the central feature of conspicuous display, and at the same time a functional space, the garden, with its ornamental porticoes, provided a direct link between the various rooms which opened onto it and became the point of convergence and living heart of the household.

2. See glossary.

Animal life on the Nile
Mosaic in the First Style.
70 x 333 cm. (28 x 131 in.).
House of the Faun, Pompeii.

This mosaic, composed of tiny coloured tesserae, decorated the floor of the threshold of the exedra, which was flanked by two coloumns separating it from the first peristyle, in the middle of which was the famous mosaic of *Alexander and Darius at the Battle of Issos*. The various animals of the Nile and its banks allude to Alexander's conquest of Egypt after the Battle of Issos.

Underwater life
Details. Mosaic in the First Style, triclinium of the House of the Faun, Pompeii.
Naples, Museo Archeologico Nazionale.

GREEK INFLUENCE IN THE SAMNITE PALACE

During the Samnite period, the house came more and more to resemble a palace in size and ostentation. If it may be said that there is no greater luxury than to dispose of a spacious house, then Pompeii offers a remarkable demonstration of the wealth of the Italic world at this time. The House of the Faun, for example, which was later embellished with a second, and even larger peristyle, rivalled the residence of a king. With its 3,000 m² (32,250 sq feet), it was vaster than the palace of Pergamum, and was surpassed in size only by the Palace of the Columns in Ptolemaïs, in Cyrenaica (present-day Libya), the residence of the Egyptian governor, which had a total area of 3,300 m² (33,100 sq feet), and the palace of a Macedonian prince in Pella, which had over 5,200 m² (55,900 sq feet). Belonging to an entirely different social and political context, the typical residences from this period are comparable only to the royal palaces and other such edifices where dynastic supremacy was officially proclaimed.

DECORATIVE SCULPTURE

The decoration of such houses provides a valuable insight into the tastes and ideology of this society of "bourgeois-princes." The usual building stone was a grey tuff from Nocera, which was as solid and durable as limestone, yet at the same time soft-grained and crumbly, and so quite easy to carve. Many stonemasons were to specialize in the carving of this local material and soon developed a high degree of skill and artistry, even mass-producing some items such as the fluted column shafts and the capitals destined to adorn private homes.

The carving of Doric capitals was facilitated by the use of a special lathe which allowed them to be produced on an "industrial" scale and sold at affordable prices. The voluted Ionic capitals, and the Corinthian capitals with their stylized acanthus leaves, had to be individually carved by experienced craftsmen. The local stonemasons soon acquired a widespread reputation, giving birth to an inventive high-quality craft tradition in the Italic region, as illustrated by the two winged sphinxes of almost calligraphic expression which probably originally guarded the entrance to a

Underwater life

Detail. Mosaic in the First Style. House VIII, 2, 16, Pompeii. Naples, Museo Archeologico Nazionale.

tomb and were later re-used to decorate a nearby country villa. The series of capitals with figures are the most interesting feature, because they integrate sculpted figurative elements into the architectural structure, as in public buildings.

PICTORIAL DECORATION: THE FIRST STYLE

Pictorial decoration in the form of murals, frescoes and mosaics provides valuable information about the tastes and cultural tendencies of the Samnite patrician caste. It often involved an iconographic programme which reflected the ideological orientation of the patron who commissioned it.

The style of mural painting in Pompeian houses evolved noticeably over the course of time, normally in in response to changing social conditions and aspirations. August Mau subdivided the murals according to different styles corresponding to the different historical phases of the city. The First Style, which he called "structural," was predominant during the Samnite Period. It served as a veritable *lingua franca* at the time, shared by all the various crafts, and it spread throughout the Hellenistic world. Its primary purpose was to conceal the walls – often built using humble materials and rudimentary techniques. The wall was first rendered in stucco, then painted in such a way as to give the impression that it had a definite architectural structure, built out of of carefully carved blocks of stone. It is not uncommon to find examples of this first mural style applying such a principle in less ostentatious homes, which might suggest that it was fashionable among well-to-do Pompeians. A quite novel phenomenon, however, can then be witnessed: whereas the wall decoration was originally used to create an architectural effect, it subsequently – and in a totally autonomous manner – developed a completely original formal idiom tending from the organic to the abstract, or, more precisely, from illusionism to "allusionism."

The Pompeian merchants who sailed the seas of the Hellenized Orient and came into contact with highly developed cultures were evidently interested in growing rich from their trade, but also in assimilating new customs and traditions. In this way, they were inspired to recreate in their own homes columned patios and gracious rooms where friends could discuss philosophy and indulge in lengthy banquets. Yet, although they were able to

enlarge their houses and give them the appearance of the royal residences that they had seen during their travels, they were unable to match the splendour of the marblework found in the latter; marble was practically inexistent in Italy then and impossible to import in sufficient quantity. Besides, there was no local labour skilled in working with such material. This led to the idea of imitating it by painting the stucco with the characteristic striped and veined patterns of different types of marble. The colour and effect of the marble combined to create a dense and rigorously geometric composition; running along the walls above a dark-coloured base, they formed a dado of large panels above which were disposed the horizontal blocks of the illusionistic stone masonry. The designs overlapped the corners, running continuously from one wall to the next, creating an enveloping effect and giving an impression of displaced reality, which would become one of the characteristic features of the future Pompeian fresco styles. Above the imitation blocks, sometimes high up on the wall, there was a forcefully projecting white stucco cornice, which, as in the case of the House of Julius Polybius (I, 13, 3), culminated in an illusionistic loggia complete with stucco pilasters. These elements accentuated the majestic appearance, emphasizing the vertical axis and adding elegantly to the real architectural design. In the two peristyles of the House of the Faun, for example, can be seen two bands of blocks flanked by pilasters running along the entire upper section of the walls, rhythmically counterbalancing the columns of the portico and creating an impression of expanded space. Such effects anticipated the taste for trompe l'oeil which came to the fore in the Second Style.

Similarly, echoing the living flowers and plants decorating the centre of the gardens, the friezes of vine stems and branches on the walls seem to wish to extend the luxuriant natural life which has been captured within the walls of the house.

PAVEMENTS AND MOSAICS

Although the strict architectural plan had excluded figurative representation from the walls, this was given free rein on the floors. Instead of the packed earth or lava paving stones which decorated ordinary houses and which were sometimes laid out in

geometric patterns, the nobler dwellings were adorned with splendid mosaicwork, or *opus vermiculatum*, one of the marvels of the Hellenizing decorative tradition. The mosaic surfaces were framed with ornate black and white patterns or borders full of rich and varied ornamental designs. In the centre, there were polychrome emblematic figures made up of tiny pieces of different-sized glass, sometimes no more than one millimeter wide. In some cases, these splendid mosaics reproduced famous Hellenistic pictorial compositions, complete with all their chromatic shades and nuances.

Once again, the House of the Faun provides the most famous and interesting examples of this art form. The rooms of the masters of the house and their guests were all decorated with magnificent mosaics: a picture of a kitten clutching a bird in its jaws, scenes of life along the banks of the Nile, a depiction of *Dionysus Riding a Panther*, and an incomparable tableau of marine fauna which could almost be a catalogue of the best-known species. With its stark contrasts, subtly balanced and delicately poetic colour-scheme, this last mosaic is an absolute masterpiece. Almost the entire floor area of the exedra opening onto the first peristyle is taken up by a huge mosaic representing Alexander the Great's victory over Darius at Issos and composed of some two million tesserae. With its twin Corinthian columns on the façade, this peristyle is undoubtedly one of the most impressive spaces in the house. The bronze *Dancing Faun* which graces the impluvium of the "public" atrium is a little masterpiece of Greek art which may have been acquired elsewhere before being brought to Pompeii. As for the unusually large and complex mosaic just mentioned, it is hardly conceivable that it was not executed *in situ*, probably by highly specialized craftsmen brought in especially from Alexandria or Sicily. This work, most certainly a copy of some famous classical painting, gives some idea of the expense involved in such large-scale mosaics, and affords a glimpse also of the very high level attained by Greek painting.

The owner of the House of the Faun was probably a member of the Satrii family, of Samnite origin, in a position, within the restricted circle of his friends, to make a conspicuous display of his assimilation of Greek culture and to assert himself both as a man of the world and as an important figure in post-Alexandrian society. In the eyes of his fellow citizens he was, and remained,

Doves
Details. Mosaic in the Second Style.
113 x 113 cm. (44 x 44 in.).
House of the Mosaic Doves, Pompeii.

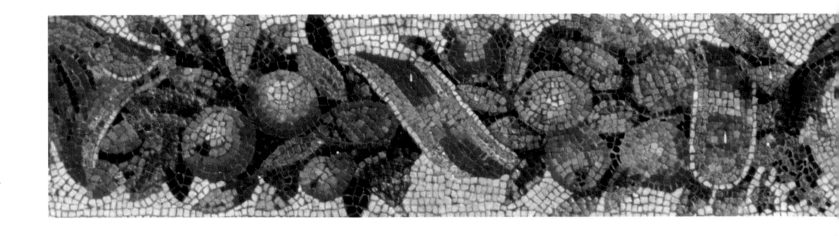

first and foremost a magistrate, and a reminder of his high-ranking position was provided by a different decoration on the floors of the public reception rooms.

The vestibule, impluvium and tablinum, all feature geometric compositions of coloured stone lozenges and triangles known as *opus sectile* which create a perspective effect. In particular, in the tablinum, the juxtaposed coloured marble, slate and green limestone lozenges are arranged in such a way as to represent cubes seen in perspective and are framed by mosaics made of large tesserae. This particular type of pavement, called *scutulatum*, was also used to decorate the floors of the *cellae* in the temples of Apollo and Jupiter in Pompeii. It is therefore not surprising to discover such a pavement in the room of the house where the magistrate, seated on his stool of office, granted audiences to the public. The sacred nature of his function was thus clearly identifiable even in a place which itself was not officially intended to be sacred. The *luxus* that was so roundly condemned by "right-thinking" moralists thus became a means of stressing the dignity and solemnity of power, and in doing so itself acquired acceptance.

It is no coincidence that a residence like the House of the Faun, even though at that time of a fairly common design, was found specifically in Pompeii. Samnite society, which had reaped substantial economic and political benefits from its alliance with Rome, had by then undergone a considerable degree of romanization. Since it maintained closer and more natural ties with the Greek world than with Rome, it's influence on the former was all the more direct. Thanks to such close cultural exchanges, the remarkable blossoming of Pompeii in the second century B.C.continued long after.

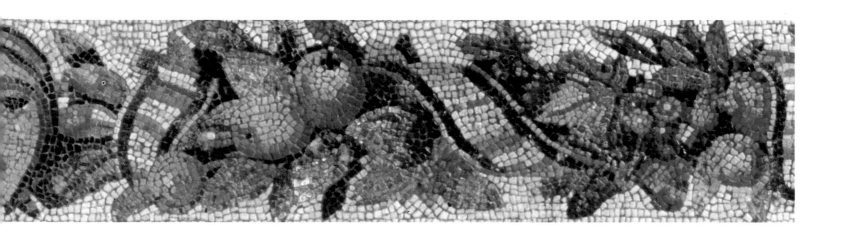

THE NEW
ROMAN SOCIETY

Architectural view with villa
Detail.

With the colonial conquest in 80 B.C., Pompeii – already extensively romanized and having adopted Latin as its official language – was politically and administratively annexed to Rome, like the other Italic cities. The old local patrician families were ousted from their positions of power by Sulla and replaced by colonists. A passage in Cicero recounts the discrimination resulting from the establishment of these newcomers who, unlike the old indigenous families, had the rank of Roman citizen. In the vestibule of the house of the priest Amandus (I, 7, 7), there is a fresco representing a battle scene; next to the depiction of a man on horseback is the name of Spartacus written in Oscan, the former language of Pompeii. Spartacus, a former gladiator, is famous for having led a desperate, ultimately unsuccessful, uprising against the Roman occupants, firing the aspiration to freedom shared by many Pompeians. As an exemplary punishment to discourage further acts of resistance, six thousand of the rebellious slaves were crucified along the Via Appia between Capua and Rome.

In the previous century, Rome had discovered in the enlightened Scipio family respected, upright mediators who managed to open up old Roman society, still rooted in the traditional rural world, to the influence of the more refined Greek culture. By the end of the Republican Period, Rome had become the most cosmopolitan city in the Ancient world, which by then had come almost completely under Roman military and political control.

To an outside observer, it would have been difficult to detect the signs of this sudden transformation in Pompeian society. Nor can it be explained entirely as a normal cultural development, for Pompeii had been forcibly merged with a wider cultural tradition. As has been shown, it was the context – or framework – in which these changes were effected that had been profoundly altered.

The "buying" of votes through acts of public largesse was an increasingly widespread phenomenon. For example, in 70 B.C., M. Porcius and C. Quintius Valgus, two faithful allies of Sulla and leading Pompeian political figures, commissioned an ampitheatre for the city built at their own expense. By lending their support to the Roman general's politics, they had adroitly strengthened their own positions and generally furthered their own interests in Campania. Only a few years before, they had already built a theatre, the *odeum* – at public expense this time – and Porcius, along with with other magistrates, had contributed to the altar in the Temple of Apollo. Such acts of conspicuous generosity, considered part of their public duties in any case, were doubtless not entirely unconnected with the appointment of censors by the central administration.

These two magistrates had the responsibility of drawing up the lists of citizens eligible to sit in the senate. It may be assumed that they included the names of men who were favourable to Pompey, then the leading political figure in Rome, and that they expected favours from them in return. For this, however, they required the full support of the populace.

In the aftermath of colonization, many Roman aristocrats settled in Pompeii and the surrounding area. The attractive Campanian countryside provided the ideal setting for the "villa life" which satisfied their increasingly felt need to compensate the frantic pace of *negotium* – the bustling political life of the city – by balancing this with *otium*, or time devoted to leisurely conversation, reflexion, and conviviality. Many of the villas originally built in the region around Pompeii by Samnite families changed hands and were converted and expanded, while new ones were built every day. In the city itself, new houses were built along the now-obsolete battlements on the south-western slope

**House of the Gems,
or of the Precious Stone**
View of the villa. 1st cent. A.D.
Herculaneum.

Architectural view with villa

Fresco in the Third Style.
22 x 53 cm. (9 x 21 in.).
Pompeii.
Naples, Museo Archeologico
Nazionale.

and beyond the city walls, facing the vast panoramic view of the Gulf of Naples.

A NEW TYPE OF HOUSE

The architecture of these new houses broke with the traditional layout according to which atrium, tablinum and peristyle were disposed along a central axis. The new dispositions and functions of the rooms and interior spaces were adapted instead to the more informal and leisurely lifestyle of the Roman villa. For reasons of conspicuous display, the atrium, the transition zone between the public and private worlds, retained its majestic proportions, but it lost its role as the focal point of family life. It was furnished with an imposing monumental entrance, while the various reception and living rooms, and sometimes even the bedrooms, looked out onto the sea or countryside. Stepped terraces – as many as four in some cases – were built in order to benefit as much as possible from the view of the gulf. The most splendid rooms had terraces built below the level of the atrium which, being at street level, was still directly exposed to the hustle and bustle of city life.

Windowless houses surrounded with high walls and completely turned inwards into private family life had by then become a thing of the past. The new architecture was generously open, with airy loggias, vast terraces and large daringly-arched windows looking out onto the nearby countryside. Nature was everywhere visible, constantly charming the senses no matter which part of the house one was in. The villas in Region VIII and the houses of the so-called *insula occidentalis* are clear examples of this new approach, a very precise image of which may be gained from the estate belonging to Fabius Rufus (VII, *ins. occ.*, 19), a member of one of the oldest Roman families. The existing city ramparts were used as foundations to elevate the house – its imposing facade built on several levels facing the sea – and offer a panoramic vantage point commanding a splendid view of the surrounding landscape. A service entrance at one end of the garden leads to the main house via a series of ramps and steps and gives access to the house directly from the port, avoiding the street. The main entrance, which gives onto a small street in the vicinity of the forum, is located on the upper level and opens onto a splendid atrium which is not surrounded by any private rooms. The street

Above

Seaside villa

Fresco in the Fourth Style.
25 x 25 cm. (10 x 10 in.).
Stabiae.
Naples, Museo Archeologico
Nazionale.

Previous pages

House of the Stags

1st cent. A.D. Herculaneum.

Terrace and belvedere overlooking
the sea.

is bordered by a long wall, the only opening in which is a service entrance which leads to the servants' quarters via a corridor running parallel to the outer wall. The reception rooms are located to the east of the atrium, while in the back, where the tablinum and living rooms would formerly have been, there is instead a series of rooms giving onto a terrace overlooking the sea.

On the first lower level there is a suite of rooms, cells, and small adjacent apartments provided with terraces and hanging gardens facing the sea. The main salon extends into a spacious *exedra*, furnished with seats for conversation. At the foot of the ramparts, outside of the city, there is another much larger garden offering a peaceful display of lush nature blooming against the deep blue backdrop of the Mediterranean.

In Herculaneum, several houses with a similar architectural design were built on the terrace above the ramparts overlooking the sea. The most typical of these is the so-called House of the Stag. The house is no longer laid out along an axis connecting the entrance and the atrium, but in line with the view of the sea. A corridor runs between the atrium and the servants' quarters, while the tablinum has been replaced by a *triclinium* oriented no longer with the entrance, but along the longitudinal axis of the house, inaugurating a new type of large, formal reception room. Indeed, laid out long this same axis is a huge garden surrounded by a series of covered porticoes, a splendid salon with a panoramic loggia. This *diaeta* is embellished by greenery on either side of a large pergola in the middle of the loggia, from which visitors could enjoy the surrounding landscape.

Whereas, at first, nature had been timidly introduced into houses with gardens, circumscribed and framed by colonnades, in this new type of house it has returned with a vengeance, as if seeking in turn to envelope and swallow up the house in its splendid panorama.

THE VILLA

The development of villas outside the city walls led to the apotheosis of nature in domestic architecture. There are many examples of seaside villas in the vicinity of Pompeii, on the hill of Varano, in Stabiae and in Oplontis, where Poppaea Sabina,

Nero's wife, owned one of the most representative houses of this genre, and in Herculaneum, where the extraordinary Villa of the Papyri stands above the coast, stretching nearly two hundred and fifty meters (two hundred and twenty yards) long. All of these residences were built on sites commanding the best view of the Gulf of Naples, but we will now turn to those villas, built by the hundreds in the fertile Vesuvian plain and at the foot of the volcano, surrounded by vineyards, orchards and fields.

In these country houses, the areas given over to farming carried out by slaves were in close, and even harmonious, proximity to the parts of the house reserved for the masters and their leisurely pursuits. Clearly intended to impress, these villas were equipped with splendid *diaetae*, and porticoes which, rather than framing an enclosed garden, opened directly out on the fields and landscapes There were also cryptoportici – ambulatories dug into the ground to provide refreshing coolness on hot summer days – exedrae, and rooms of various sizes designed to offer the right degree of comfort according to the weather, season and time of day.

EVOLUTION OF THE TOWN HOUSE

The urban residence of the wealthy Pompeian reflected the new ideals of the Roman citizen. It was no longer inspired by the architecture of Hellenistic palaces, but by the design of the villas, though indeed on a more modest scale. Wherever the opportunity arose, the rooms were enlarged to the detriment of adjacent buildings, by undertaking large-scale structural alterations which incorporated them into the main building, or simply by integrating them as separate elements into a larger complex. This latter solution was chosen for the House of the Ship "Europa" (I, 15, 1-3), the House of Menander (I, 10, 4), the House of the Gilded Amorini (VI, 16, 7), the House of Ariadne (VII, 4, 31-51), and the House of the Cryptoporticus (I, 6, 2). Another example is the House of the Citharist (I, 4, 5, 25-28), which, with the successive addition of different buildings, eventually extended over an area of 2,300 m² (24,725 sq feet) and included two atriums and three peristyles.

Elsewhere, upper floors used as servants' quarters were built above the rooms surrounding the atrium, as in the House of the

Above

Shrine for the Lares
1st cent. A.D.
Pompeii.

Opposite

Masonry walls

Top

Opus quasi reticulatum: a less refined form of the opus reticulatum (see below).
Early 1st cent. B.C. Pompeii.

Middle

Opus latericium, brick wall with circular ornament.
1st cent. A.D. Pompeii.

Below

Opus reticulatum: made of small polygonal tuff bricks, set in mortar and disposed in fairly regular rows.
Late 1st cent. A.D. Pompeii.

Silver Wedding (V, 2, i). New facilities, typical of the villa, were installed in many patrician residences. The House of Menander and the House of the Cryptoporticus, for instance, were equipped with thermal installations, allowing the inhabitants to relax intimately far from the crowded bustle of the public baths, which, even though a new establishment had been built in the forum, were often overcrowded.

PICTORIAL DECORATION AND MOSAICWORK: THE SECOND STYLE

Mural painting now sought to translate into images the refined atmosphere of the villa, a lifestyle which was not merely fashionable in Rome, but had become a veritable passion. The Roman aristocracy brought a new pictorial style to Pompeii which became as characteristic of this period as the construction of walls with "*quasi-reticulatum*" facing, i.e. with small polygonal tuff bricks sealed into the cement in rows to form regular patterns.

The Second Style, the origins of which reach back to the Hellenistic Orient, developed in the Roman world along the lines anticipated by the architecture of the First Style. Now, however, relying solely on painting, it covered the walls with columns, porticoes and niches, creating an illusion of extended space while concealing the wall surfaces with trompe-l'œil architectural perspectives or scenes depicting animals, human figures, tableaux or symbolic objects. Occasionally small theatres are re-created, with lifesize figures performing the sacred mysteries; others are so realistically rendered that even to the modern spectator, no matter how uninitiated or blasé, they seem to be allegories of life itself. One great admirer of these "images of all that is and can be" was Vitruvius, and their incomparable pictorial and iconographic richness may be seen in the immense mural cycles in the Villa of Fannius Sinistor at Boscoreale, in the salon of the Villa of Mysteries or in the House of Oplontis.

The Pompeians, now Roman citizens both in fact and in law, were eager to assimilate the culture and ideology of the "capital of the world." They adopted the new artistic styles brought by cosmopolitan Roman aristocrats who were flocking to the countryside to escape the stresses of urban life. The Pompeian artists tried their hand at "realistic trompe-l'œil" effects, painting

Opposite

Allegory of Death

Mosaic in the Second Style.
47 x 41 cm. (18 x 16 in.).
Triclinium in workshop I, 5, 2,
Pompeii.
Naples, Museo Archeologico
Nazionale.

Below

**Plaster cast of a victim
of the eruption**

Pompeii.

The bodies of the victims were covered with layers of ash which moulded the finest details of their bodies. As the ash cooled and solidified and the bodies naturally decomposed, only a cinerite cavity was left. Plaster was injected into these cavities to obtain casts of the bodies.

Seated matron

Fresco in the Second Style.
170 x 96 cm. (67 x 38 in.).
Villa of the Mysteries, Pompeii.

This is one of the most famous works
of Roman painting, and dates
from the 1st cent. B.C. It represents
the celebration of a Dionysian mystery.
The seated woman could be a rich
matron or a priestess of Bacchus.
The famous "Pompeii red" was
obtained using minium, an alum
sulfate.

architectural elements, plinths, dais, colonnades, and so on, to give a feeling of greater depth and space to the rooms. Where once, the walls had tended to pale into insignificance in the presence of realistic-looking architectural elements, now, between the panels that composed the foreground plane, they offered glimpses of neatly ordered rows of columns and buildings, and vast landscapes fading into the distance. Through a pictorial fiction, the interior spaces of the home opened onto the outer world, or let it penetrate within; one could contemplate, as if from a villa window, vast panoramas with their calm, soft-toned, gentle spectacle of life.

The deployment of figurative elements in the murals, whether as landscape tableaux appearing through false doors, or as objects and animals (probably with allegorical meanings) integrated into the architectural compositions, led the new style to abandon the central iconic figurative motifs on the floors in favour of geometrical, often polychrome, patterns, featuring braiding, interlacing, wickerwork effects, and cubes shown in perspective, all of which were also designed to create three-dimensional illusion.

COLUMNED SALONS

At the same time, the actual space itself took on an ever more majestic aspect. In this highly competitive society, luxury became a social necessity. The salons of patrician residences such as the House of the Labyrinth, the House of the Silver Wedding, or the House of Meleager (VI, 9, 2) were filled with veritable forests of columns – real ones, this time – which combined their perspective effects with those of the illusory architecture painted on the walls. These *oeci*, or reception rooms, were invested with an official character. No pains were spared to create an atmosphere intended to inspire respect for civic virtues and to endow these rooms with a quasi-sacred character, similar to that of the basilica, the loftiest expression of public architecture in the Roman world. Even within the confines of his home, the owner's public life and function were displayed and emphasized. Emulating the Greek dynasties, he strove to present an image of himself as cultured, refined citizen, yet never forgetting to mention the burden of duties and responsibilities that accompanied his role in the community.

TUFF SCULPTURE

As far as tuff sculpture was concerned, the new generation of stonemasons still drew its inspiration from the old local traditions of Greek origin. At the *odeum*, or Little Theatre, they carved the admirable kneeling telamons at the foot of the walls surrounding the *cavea*, and the two superb winged paws of wild animals – remarkable for their strong graphic effect – at each end of the balustrade that separated the *proedria* from the *cavea*. Here again, the sculpture complements the architecture, as is the case with the forceful terracotta telamons, hands folded above their heads, which support the architrave of the vaultof the *tepidarium* in the Forum baths and, at the same time, frame a series of niches placed along the walls, creating a fine chiaroscuro effect.

LITERARY CULTURE

During the colonial period, Pompeii succeeded in integrating itself completely into the Roman world. The two cities remained so closely related ideologically and culturally that the findings of archaeological excavations over the centuries and literary sources were to be mutually enlightening. Much of our knowledge of Roman art, life and thought is inextricably linked to the rediscovery of Pompeii in modern times.

Thus, on the walls of the city – more specifically, of the *odeum* – have been found inscriptions in verse from a poet who has even left his name: Tiburtinus. Although clearly not the work of a major poet, these fragmentary Latin verses, which may have been part of a single composition, are of considerable historical interest. They are stylistically related to Hellenistic poetry, that of Alexandria in particular, drawing on the latter's poetic structure, lyrical motifs and literary models. With the limited resources of the amateur, Tiburtinus tried his hand at a poetical form which was to lead the *neotoroi*, or "new poets", in Rome to a major rediscovery of Greek lyric verse, and to engender the sublime poems of Catullus.

Tiburtinus inscribed this "Song of Despair" on a wall in Pompeii:

*"What happened? After having drawn me helplessly
into the fire, O my eyes, now your cheeks run with tears.
But the tears cannot put out the flames
They spread across your face and darkness comes
into the spirit."*

*"If you know the power of love,
if a human heart beats in your breast, have pity on me,
let me come to you."*

*"Cesia...
eat, drink, enjoy yourself...
not always...."*

Echoing some unhappy love affair, these words seem to anticipate its futility. At the very moment of launching an invitation to enjoy the pleasures of life, they relapse into the unspeakable melancholy that springs from an awareness of the ephemeral nature of all things, projecting them on this wall that time has spared.

95

**Allegories of Persia
and Macedonia**

Details. Fresco in the Second Style.
200 x 325 cm. (79 x 128 in.).
Villa of Fannius Sinistor, Boscoreale.
Naples, Museo Archeologico
Nazionale.

The meaning of this masterpiece of Pompeian wall-painting remains
unclear. The figures of the two women have been identified
as personifications of Macedonia (detail on the left), bearing arms
after her victory over Persia, who sits pensively before her. According
to other authors, this fresco represents Antigone Gonathas,
the king of Macedonia sitting in front of his mother, Philas.

THE GOLDEN AGE OF THE FIRST IMPERIAL PERIOD

Head of the Doryphorus

Bronze. Copy signed by Apollonios
of Athens, after a Greek original
by Polykleitos. Augustan Period.
Height: 54 cm. (21 in.).
Villa of the Papyri, Herculaneum.
Naples, Museo Archeologico
Nazionale.

Opposite

Runner

Bronze. Roman copy
after a 4th cent. B.C. Greek original.
1st cent. B.C.-1st cent. A.D.
Height: 118 cm. (46 in.).
Villa of the Papyri, Herculaneum.
Naples, Museo Archeologico
Nazionale.

After the troubled years of civil war, during which Roman legions confronted and fought other Roman legions in campaigns conducted throughout the entire Ancient world, the doors of the Temple of Janus in the Forum in Rome could finally be closed again. The establishment of the Roman Empire ushered in a new era of peace. The fierce hatred that had pitted members of the same family against one another, the supporters of Caesar against those of Pompey, had finally subsided, and the times of conspiracy and assassination were no more than a faint memory. With the defeat of Mark-Antony at the Battle of Actium in 31 B.C., Octavian's triumph was indisputable. The world was his for the asking, and the Roman senate begged him to take it. Rome was weary of war, and it was urgent for the common good that the climate of internal strife come swiftly to an end. Octavian, who adopted the title of *Augustus*, was the only leader capable of consolidating the many conquests won by the invincible Roman armies. At long last, a durable peace would offer the Roman world a new era of prosperity.

The return to a mythical golden age in which, as imperial propaganda claimed, there would once again be a place for everyone, made it possible for each Roman to devote himself to the creation of a better world by participating in public works on a grand scale. The cities most closely linked to Rome were the first to benefit from the economic well-being that the opening years of the Empire brought to the entire peninsula.

As we know, imperial propaganda was also propagated through the voices of the official court poets, and it is extremely interesting to note how great their fame was in Pompeii. The measure of this phenomenon is easily taken by the number of graffiti that reproduce their verses on the walls of the city. Those of Virgil in particular were often quoted, and sometimes even parodied. The works of such poets were probably taught in the schools in order to popularize them as widely as possible among the younger generations.

THE NEW SOCIAL COMPONENTS

An increasing trend during this period was the massive emigration from far-flung cities of the Empire to the capital. The newcomers were spurred on by dreams of fortune or trade, or drawn by material and cultural incentives. Rome, which was already the home of large numbers of slaves purchased in the Orient or captured as spoils of war, became the greatest melting pot of populations that the civilized world had ever seen.

Pompeii was ideally located in the Gulf of Naples. Members of the imperial court and of the Roman aristocracy now flocked to the fabulous villas all along the coast, from Capri to the *Promontorium Minervae* (present-day Punta Campanella, near Sorrento) and Baia. Thanks to its busy port, Pompeii became the focal point of this intense flow and exchange of populations. Until the creation of the port of Ostia, Pozzuoli was the principal port of call for shipments destined for Rome. As Strabo, the Greek geographer who wrote under Augustus, reminds us, the position of the port, at the midpoint of the gulf, opening onto the plain behind and offering easy access to the hinterland with its prosperous towns such as Nola, Nocera and Acerra, made Pompeii the pivot for trade between Campania and the Orient – especially Egypt and Alexandria.

Relations between Pompeii and Alexandria had already been very close since the Samnite Period, as attested by the construction of a Temple of Isis (where sacred water from the Nile was preserved) near the Grand Theatre in the late 2nd. Century B.C., and by the settlement of an Alexandrian community at the foot of

Above

Private fountain

Polychrome tesserae. 1st cent. B.C.
House of the Small Fountain, Pompeii.

This fountain, the shape of which evokes that of a grotto, stands against a wall at the foot of a garden. The wall is decorated with murals of grandiose landscapes in the Fourth Style.
The fountain itself is decorated with seashell inlays. Two bronze statuettes representing a cupid and a fisherman stand on the floor. The originals are in the Naples museum.

Opposite

Children with geese and bunches of grapes

Bronze. 1st cent. A.D.
House of the Vettii, Pompeii.

Vesuvius during this same period. With the conquest of Egypt by Augustus, ties between these two cities took on a new importance. Alexandria was a source not only of luxury products like works of art and perfumes, but also of the grain supplies that were so necessary to the Empire. It can be imagined that such highly organized exchanges were conducted in the flourishing port of Pompeii, with ships constantly docking and sailing, and merchants running their trading posts.

The mostly Greek-speaking foreigners arriving in Pompeii in increasing numbers during the Imperial Period profoundly modified the social and economic activities of the city. One only has to see the names of the residents and the great quantities of graffiti written in Greek, or using Greek expressions, to get an idea of the proportionately large number of inhabitants of Hellenic origin in Pompeii.

Whereas the old Samnite families had accumulated their wealth through agriculture rather than commerce, the new economic leaders, many of whom were emancipated slaves, made their fortunes in commerce, public and private construction, and "industry."

MIDDLE-CLASS HABITAT

A wealth of irrefutable sources allow us to form a fairly precise idea of the type of housing and lifestyle enjoyed by the lower classes at the beginning of the Empire. Archaeology, however, proves to be of little help in this case, because the houses in which the humblest Pompeians lived during the previous period were – precisely because they were of such simple construction – constantly undergoing renovation and rebuilding; because of this it is difficult to rely on the vestiges preserved by the eruption.

Although the members of the middle class had limited financial resources, they were nonetheless concerned with appearances and respectability, and they did not shrink from equipping their houses with an atrium, no matter how modest its size. An example of this may be seen in the House of Amandio (I, 7, 3) which, although possessing a total floor area of barely 127 m² (1,365 sq feet), manages to create the illusion of a veritable garden. Of the houses with a floor area between 120 and

Resting Hermes
Bronze. Roman copy after a Greek
original by Lysippos.
1st cent. B.C.-1st cent. A.D.
Height: 115 cm. (45 in.).
Main peristyle of the Villa of the
Papyri, Herculaneum.
Naples, Museo Archeologico
Nazionale.

150 m² (1,290 and 1,610 sq feet), ten feature an atrium. The number increases to twenty-nine for the similarly-sized houses with an upper story and an altogether different layout plan. If the houses of between 50 and 150 m² (540 and 1,610 sq feet) are taken into consideration, the total number of atriums rises to eighty-three.

These houses belonged to people whose social status and function did not require formal reception rooms, and who were thus free to lay out the interior spaces as they wished. These dwellings were sometimes located in a block behind other houses with façades onto the street. They had very irregular floor-plans; the various rooms opened onto a long corridor, and the courtyards served as air shafts and light wells. The inhabitable spaces were arranged around a garden and were used according to the tastes and needs of the occupants, without any overt concern for show.

It is not to be imagined, however, that all of these houses without atriums were small. Many of them were fairly large, as large as houses with an atrium, and some as big as 600 and even 800 m² (6,450 and 8,600 sq feet). Not to mention those which had cultivated fields behind, and which might easily cover 1,000 to 1,500 m² (10,750 and 16,100 sq feet), some even as much as 2,500 m² (26,875 sq feet).

Although the size of the house remained an indication of the owners' wealth, it was no longer closely related to any need for conspicuous display. Without seeking to establish a too systematic – and doubtless incorrect – correspondence between the type and floor area of these houses, and the owners' social origin, it could be said that this phenomenon was linked to the assimilation of immigrants into Pompeian society throughout the first Imperial Period. These foreigners or emancipated slaves, with relatively modest social ambitions, merged naturally into the humble populace of craftsmen, peasants, and small shopkeepers.

Other dwellings were characterized by the presence of an upper story. The trend towards building upwards began during the Republican Period and became increasingly popular during the years of the Empire right up to the city's very last years. This additional floor was often built inside the house – whether with, or without an atrium – to meet the needs of the *familia*, or could be laid out into one or more small, independent apartments, or

Pseudo-Seneca

Bronze bust. Roman copy
after a Hellenistic original.
1st cent. B.C.-1st cent. A.D.
Height: 33 cm. (13 in.).
Main peristyle of the Villa
of the Papyri, Herculaneum.
Naples, Museo Archeologico
Nazionale.

This bust has been traditionally
identified as a likeness of the
philosopher Seneca.

Dancers

Bronze. Mid-1st cent. B.C.
Height: 153, 155, 151, 150 and 146 cm.
(from 57 to 61 in.).
Villa of the Papyri, Herculaneum.
Naples, Museo Archeologico
Nazionale.

This group of five female figures was
placed along the *euripe*, and is thought
to represent dancers. They are more
likely figures of *hydrophorai*, or water
bearers. These bronzes are local
renditions of classical Greek statues.

cenacula, which communicated directly with the street or an inner courtyard via a flight of stairs. This type of housing, which was very common in the centre of town, consisted of a series of two or three successive rooms connected by galleries or balconies, and provided very comfortable living spaces for its occupants, generally tenants. Although there were many such dwellings, few have been preserved in their entirety, for their floors and roofs easily collapsed under the weight of the volcanic hail. The vestiges of the more luxurious of such houses often feature traces of the niches made in the walls for bedspace, decorative murals, comfortably-sized rooms, and good lighting, showing that the owners were not a little concerned with displaying their good taste. A small inscription has been found advertising the rental of *cenacula* in the *insula Arriana Polliana*, where the House of Pansa (VI, 6, 1), one of the largest *domi* from the Samnite Period, is also located. The lodgings are qualified as *equestria*, i.e. suitable for members of the knighthood. Although common sense dictates that not too much credence should be lent to such misleading "salestalk", and even if there is no way of verifying the credibility of this advertisement, it nevertheless clearly points to the reputation for comfort associated with this type of dwelling.

In a different vein was the *pergula*, a sort of closet, or mezzanine, generally made of wood and built above a small shop, or *taberna*, to which it was connected by a small inside staircase. The day's work over, the shopkeeper could retire upstairs to bed. These tiny rooms – usually no larger than a few sq meters – enabled less well-off people, or in other words, a large segment of the population, to have a place of their own, however small, in which to live and work. During the day, the *taberna* opened onto the streetfront to display the wares, and at night it could be closed by sliding a series of planks into especially-carved grooves in the floor and architrave to form a kind of barrier. A small door cut into the planks allowed entry and exit; in this way, the shop could easily be converted into a living space, and in the upstairs closet there was enough room for a mat or mattress for a good night's rest.

Pompeians who lacked a fireplace to cook their meals could eat at the many *thermopolia* and *cauponae*, if not at the homes of the "nouveaux riches" who, always eager to flaunt their newly-earned wealth, were constantly surrounded by a swarm of spongers. It was therefore not particularly difficult to get invited somewhere

Villa of the Papyri

The Villa of the Papyri, located on the seacoast
not far from Herculaneum, is a perfect example
of a vacation villa belonging to members of the Roman
aristocracy at the end of the Republican Period. In
addition to a very rich library of philosophical works –
mostly of Epicurean tendency – the villa boasted
a collection of indoor and outdoor statues (58 in bronze,
21 in marble), providing a good illustration of the tastes
of cultivated Romans at the time.

for a hot meal. Two graffiti found in the basilica give some idea of the extent of such a practice which, for many impoverished Pompeians, not only offered the pleasure of dining in company, but was a veritable means of daily survival. The first inscription declares: "Good health to whosoever invites me to lunch," while the second is directly addressed by name to a braggart who failed to keep his promise: "What a prig that Lucius Istacidius is, not inviting me to supper!"

There was yet another type of dwelling providing work and living space for craftsmen and small shopkeepers. These combined shops and houses were larger and more comfortable than the *pergulae*, and so better suited to family life. The shopfront once again was largely open to the street, but the shop itself had one or more back rooms, occasionally an interior courtyard providing air and light, and in some cases even an upper story. These dual-purpose houses located in the centre of town, along the busiest streets, probably already existed during the Samnite Period, although, as we have said, none of the remaining dwellings of this type date from so far back.

Often, examples of all of the above-described types of dwellings are to be found within the same block Thus, we see impressive dwellings with an atrium standing next to *pergulae*, shop-dwellings, and *cenacula.*, mingling a variety of social classes with their differing standards of living within the same neighbourhood.

THE DEVELOPMENT OF THE PATRICIAN HOUSES AND THE GARDEN

Other than the ornamental use of the marble that was now being quarried at Luni and shipped in large quantities to Campania, where it found its way into most of the impluviums installed in Pompeii, the most remarkable development in the homes of the upper classes, with their atriums and peristyles, was the possibility of piped fresh running water channelled down to Pompeii via the Serino aqueduct. Public fountains in the streets now provided water for the houses which lacked rainwater cisterns. The houses with an atrium could be connected up to the public water supply providing the owner bore the expenses involved.

Irrigation was thus made easier, and people vied with their neighbours to create yet more beautiful gardens. In the garden belonging to Julius Polybius, the roots of four large fruit trees have been found. Fruit trees used to be among the basic features of the oldest gardens, and were apparently preserved as an elegant sign of the venerable age of the garden and the ancient origins of the family that owned it. It became a fashionable preoccupation at the time to lay out lawns and to plant flowers and shrubs so as obtain the most harmonious possible succession of floral displays.

FOUNTAINS AND NYMPHAEA

The arrival of running water was a godsend for Pompeians striving to emulate, as far as this was possible in an urban setting, the comforts and luxury of the nearby villas. In summer, the Roman emperors and nobles customarily repaired to special grottoes, or *nymphaea*, more often than not built on the seacoast. These grottoes were enhanced by lapping crystal-clear springs, beautiful statues and works of art. Here, the nobles could escape the heat of the afternoon hours, indulging in esthetic pursuits. The Grotta Azzura and Grotta Matromania in Capri, and the one at Sperlonga are the best-known examples. Then people began to create imitations of such grottoes in the city itself, laying out nymphaea – splendid constructions the principal feature of which is water falling down a series of tiered cascades into a pool. The artificial grotto in the House of the Centenary is by far the most grandiose one of its kind. The *triclinium-nymphaea* – richly decorated marble affairs to be seen at the House of Julia Felix (II, 4, 3) and at the House of the Golden Bracelet (VI, *ins. occ.*, 42) – combined the image of the grotto with that of the *stibadium*, a sort of outdoor summer triclinium.

If for some reason the construction of a real nymphaeum proved unfeasible, elaborate fountains equipped with grotto-like niches were built and decorated with seashells and splendid polychrome glass mosaics. The Houses of the Large and Small Fountain, the House of the Wounded Bear (VII, 2, 45), the House of the Scientists (VI, 14, 43) and the House of the Golden Bracelet feature a variety of these spectacular creations.

With the availability of a plentiful supply of water it became possible to decorate gardens with springs and fountains of all

kinds: dolphins spouting water, large basins supported by cupids, or grimacing masks made of bronze or marble, all modelled on the inexhaustible repertory of Greek statuary.

SCULPTURE IN THE HOUSE AND GARDEN

Gardens became veritable outdoor art galleries comparable to those that could be seen in the villas of the wealthy collectors of the day, constantly in search of the finest works of Greek art, for which they were prepared to pay incredibly high prices. The garden paths were lined with columns and pedestals displaying herms, masks, statues of Bacchus, Venus, Hercules, Eros and various woodland deities. The most outstanding of these garden-galleries is undoubtedly the one at the Villa of the Papyri in Herculaneum. Other notable examples of garden statuary may be seen at the House of the Vettii (VI, 15, 1), the House of the Gilded Amorini, the House of the Citharist and the House of Marcus Lucretius (IX, 3, 5). At the house of Octavius Quartio (II, 2 2), who, like Fabius Rufus, dispensed with enclosing porticoes and made the garden more open to the surrounding landscape, the statues were placed in the Egyptian manner, along the banks of a long canal, or *euripe*, which crossed the vast gardens and was supposed to symbolize the life-bringing waters of the Nile. It matters little that most of these artworks in Pompeii are mere copies, for the most part mass-produced. Sculpture had become an indispensable part of the decoration of gardens and grottoes, as painting had long been so in the case of domestic interiors. At any rate, it is still difficult to get an idea of the personality and culture of the owners of a particular house merely by analyzing of the elements of its decoration. Such attempts can be very misleading, for the "works of art" on display often bore little relation to art in the nobler sense, and even less to the actual artistic culture of the owners. They were merely often superficial expressions of their owners' personal tastes, which, as we shall see, were not always of the most refined sort. It must be said that the Romans – unlike the Greeks in this respect – although generally quite sensitive in esthetic matters, never reached the point of assigning to art an absolute spiritual value, the idea of art for art's sake. They could appreciate the decorative and functional aspects of art, and even more the fact

Opposite, top

Cup with stylized leaves
Silver. 1st cent. A.D.
Height: 8 cm. (3 in.).
Diam. 13.4 cm. (5 in.).
Region around Vesuvius.
Naples, Museo Archeologico
Nazionale.

Bottom

Small gourd
Silver. 1st cent. A.D.
Height: 15 cm. (6 in.).
Diam. 11.2 cm. (4 in.).
Pompeii.
Naples, Museo Archeologico
Nazionale.

Below

Tray
Silver. Mid-1st cent. A.D.
59.5 x 40.5 cm. (23 x 16 in.).
Herculaneum.
Naples, Museo Archeologico
Nazionale.

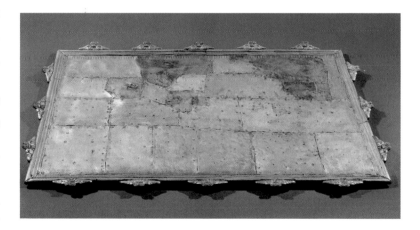

that its presence in a house considerably enhanced the owner's prestige. Not even some of the more prominent cultural figures of the day were free of this very pedestrian notion of art. Thus, Cicero, for example, wrote to Atticus asking him to look for some some bas-reliefs on the art-market merely to decorate the sides of a small atrium. Not surprisingly, therefore, we can find in the houses of wealthy Pompeians lifesize bronze statues – probably copies of Greek masterpieces – used as torch-holders to light the triclinium during banquets. Examples of these are the *lychnophoroi* found in the House of Fabius Rufus, the House of Julius Polybius and in the House of the Ephebe (I, 7, 11). In other cases, we see original pieces belonging to the Alexandrian art tradition, like the figures of cake vendors, or *placentarii*, found in the House of the Ephebe, which were simply used as plate holders to present food. For almost diametrically opposed reasons, it is not rare to find finely sculpted marble high-reliefs, or paws of wild animals carved almost in the round, together with ordinary bas-reliefs of rinceaux, volutes and acanthus leaves, splendidly decorating the tables and *cartibula*, which were placed respectively in the garden and in the atrium.

Female portrait
Fresco in the Third Style.
41 x 26 cm. (16 x 10 in.).
Herculaneum.
Naples, Museo Archeologico Nazionale.

HERMS AND STATUES

More original and interesting from the artistic point of view were the bronze or marble portrait-busts that could now be seen in the atriums of patrician houses. They evolved out of funerary art, and realism in the purest Italic tradition that had been pressed into the service of republican ideals and personality cults. In the new imperial and colonial context they expressed a sense of civic pride and prestige similar to that emanating from the statues of meritorius citizens in the forum and other public places.

The marble herms in the house of Cornelius Rufus (VIII, 4, 15) and the House of Orpheus (VI, 14, 20), and the bronze busts in the house of Caecilius Jucundus (V, 1, 26), all highly visible signs of distinction, were placed there for honorific purposes and express the gratitude of the *familia*.

In the Temple of Eumachios, we can see the statue of the priestess erected by the fullers in honour of their patron-goddess. The so-called statue of Livia – in fact another priestess – in the

Villa of Mysteries is dedicated to the memory of a member of the illustrious *gens* Istacidia which owned the house. These last two statues display the classicizing folds and hairstyles which the women of the imperial family had made fashionable in Rome.

LUXURY CURIOS

This thirst for wealth and its conspicuous display, as well as the constant search for social approval, often found expression in the minor arts, in works produced by highly skilled craftsmen and which were in great demand among collectors. Precious objects like silverware – which is to a house what jewelry is to a body – were taken out on special occasions and for banquets as a mark of prestige. An abundance of gold and silver objects, especially tableware, was one of the most highly prized external signs of wealth, and was intended to reflect the hosts' good taste and economic status. Petronius, the "arbiter of elegance" at Nero's court, described this passion for luxury at great length in his famous *Satyricon*. To mention only one episode: at the entrance to the house of Trimalcion, his unforgettable "nouveau-riche" hero, he describes the concièrge busily shelling peas into a silver plate.

Glass, a less noble yet widespread material, often imitated the designs of the tableware of the nobles, and glassmakers created such masterpieces as the "Blue Vase", decorated with glass cameos of cupids harvesting grapes amid rinceaux and vine branches, or the glass chalices from Stabiae that imitate the translucence of obsidian, decorated with relief figures of Egyptian design made of inlaid gems, colourful coral and gold filigree. Pieces of silverware have been found in many Pompeian houses, including two remarkable collections of entire sets. One came from the House of the Menander and included 118 pieces; the other, which consisted of 109 pieces, from the Villa della Pisanella in Boscoreale. Both sets featured objects from different periods, ranging from the closing years of the Republic down to Nero's time, with a large number of pieces dating from the Augustan period. The figurative motifs were inspired by mythological, dionysiac, naturalistic, philosophical or allegorical themes. The goldsmiths, some of whom were surely of Roman or Campanian origin, applied their amazing mastery of chasing

Medallion with a young man
Fresco in the Fourth Style.
28 x 22 cm. (11 x 9 in.).
Herculaneum.
Naples, Museo Archeologico
Nazionale.

and repoussé techniques to traditional Greek designs. These dish-warmers, braziers, candlesticks, lanterns, cake moulds, tableware sets and other bronze objects, some with remarkably fine relief decoration, clearly contributed to the image of the house, displaying a luxury which, independently of the whims of fashion, had become an indispensable factor of social prestige.

PICTORIAL DECORATION: THE THIRD STYLE

Already during the Republican Period, the Second Style had undergone noticeable transformations, moving progressively away from the tromple-l'œil realism of architectural views. The elements became more discreet and seemed to tend more towards specifically pictorial values, independent of realistic representation. The perspective views of buildings and colonnades which used to occupy the central zones of the panels now gave way to properly pictorial scenes, while the decorative architectural elements acted rather as frames. The walls, which previously had been concealed by the illusory painting, became the main support for an autonomous, ornamental and fantastic pictorial expression in which columns turned into plant stems or candlesticks, while the spaces were divided up and arranged in definite hierarchy.

One noteworthy contemporary, the architect Vitruvius, expressed his dismay and incomprehension at this new style: "The walls are no longer being painted with the real images of things that we know, but rather with things that make no sense (*monstrum*): instead of columns, we see fluted stems with withered leaves and vine branches; instead of pediments, imitation arabesques; and there are candlelabras holding pictures of miniature temples on the pediments of which one sees tiny flowers and figurines placed without rhyme or reason on bushes with volutes. Or there are plant stems ending in half-figures, or heads of animals and human beings. Well, these things do not exist, cannot exist, never have existed. How can a reed support a roof, a candlelabra the ornaments of a pediment?"

To be sure, the values and elements of the decorative code used in painting to define and hierarchize the social function of the places it was called upon to to embellish were by then

Medallion with young woman
Fresco in the Fourth Style.
28 x 22 cm. (11 x 9 in.).
Herculaneum.
Naples, Museo Archeologico
Nazionale.

Bacchus and Maenad

Fresco in the Fourth Style.
36 x 37 cm. (14 x 15 in.).
Provenance unknown.
Naples, Museo Archeologico
Nazionale.

"Sappho"

Fresco in the Fourth Style.
31 x 31 cm. (12 x 12 in.).
Region VI, *insula occidentalis*, Pompeii.
Naples, Museo Archeologico
Nazionale.

This figure of a young woman
is shown holding the attributes of an
educated person: a stylus and a booklet
composed of wax tablets.
Her hair is held in place by a golden
hair-net, a fashion from the time of
Nero, and her large gold ear-rings
show that she belongs to a rich family.
The slight strabismus is one of Venus'
characteristic features. The portrait of
this young woman was accompanied
by that of her husband shown holding
a volume of Plato's works.

Hercules finds his son Telephus in Arcadia
Detail of Hercules. Fresco in the Fourth Style.
218 x 182 cm. (86 x 72 in.).
Basilica, Herculaneum.
Naples, Museo Archeologico Nazionale.

generally acknowledged. Painting could therefore move away from descriptive representations of reality and simply allude to it, while developing a language of its own, this time purely symbolic. Everyone was aware of the allegorical significance of a column, and so it did not have to be represented realistically on the wall in order for its function to be clearly legible. It could therefore be transformed symbolically, according to purely formal principles, into a plant stem or a candlelabra. Freed from the tyranny imposed by imitative architectural representation, painting could now develop its own autonomous figurative idiom.

This led to the birth and growth of the Third Style, the most innovative and also probably the most beautiful of the four painting styles. The wall was divided, according to a precise decorative syntax, into three distinct areas: a base, central, and upper zone. This articulation of the wall surface had already been present in the previous styles, but it had now become a conventional form of expression. Each wall had a pictorial identity of its own and was related to the whole only through an interplay of formal correspondences. The architectural elements represented in the central – and most important – zone moved towards the centre to create an *aedicula*, a mere pretext to draw the gaze to a figurative scene, often a subject drawn from Greek mythology, which was the focal point of the composition. It was here that the artist, or *pictor imaginarius*, could demonstrate his skill. These frescoes, which sometimes belonged to a single thematic programme throughout the house, are among the most beautiful examples of ancient painting that have come down to us. Yet they are merely "documents" giving us an overall idea of the pictorial culture of the ancient Romans. There is little spontaneous creativity to be seen, for the painters copied the scenes from a vast repertoire of "cartoons" which they interpreted and modified according to their ability, or the prevailing influences. Although rather cold from the spiritual point of view, these paintings impress us with their forceful colour-schemes, the scenes they depict, the ideas they express, and the world they evoke. The pleasure we derive from them is emotional and intellectual rather esthetic and spiritual, but it is nonetheless a pleasure of rare intensity.

The paintings preserved in many houses in Pompeii, especially the larger ones, like those in the House of the Citharist, in the

cells of the House of Fatal Love (IX, 5, 18-21), or those in the triclinium of the Villa Imperiale, have today become major reference-points in the cultural history of Western painting. On either side of the aedicula, the wall surface was subdivided into panels painted in a uniform ground and dotted with finely painted ornaments, in the centre of which were vignettes featuring figures or landscapes, often painted with an "impressionistic" handling and bearing no direct relationship with the other pictorial elements on the wall.

The architecture in the upper zone became miniaturized, while the arabesques, rinceaux, and volutes of the plant motifs that had become an integral part of the ornamental repertoire expressed an absolute denial of real space. The prevailing fashion called for simple ornamental compositions with small panels representing landscapes or still lifes, masks, and fantastic figures; all these figures, of every imaginable form, were harmoniously disposed in a rigidly and rationally organized pictorial space.

Egypt, which had become the Roman emperor's personal property after his victory at Actium, seemed to be a favourite source of inspiration for the Pompeian artists. Many paintings depicted its venerable and mysterious deities, which had long been assimilated into the Roman pantheon, along with landscapes of the Nile, pygmies and exotic animals. The taste for Egyptian culture, an inexhaustible model for interior decoration, had become more than just a fashion, but a veritable craze.

The demand for simplicity led to interiors with an atmosphere of great refinement. These elegant decors were matched by floor mosaics laid out in very plain, geometric patterns, often in alternating black and white elements. Polychromy and effects of illusionistic depth were rejected. Even when mosaic decoration included figurative elements, as in the house of Paquius Proculus (I, 7, 1), they were treated as simple geometric patterns.

PAINTED GARDENS

The major characteristic of the Third Style, however, was the appearance of vast pictorial cycles depicting imaginary gardens. Whether covering only one wall or taking over all of the walls of a room reserved for family use, often enhanced with ornamental marble or *tabulae pictae* which highlighted the intimate character

Theseus and the Minotaur
Detail. Fresco in the Fourth Style.
194 x 155 cm. (76 x 61 in.).
Basilica, Herculaneum.
Naples, Museo Archeologico
Nazionale.

Pensive woman

Fresco in the Fourth Style.
53 x 49 cm. (21 x 19 in.).
Villa of Ariadne, Stabiae.
Naples, Museo Archeologico
Nazionale.

of such rooms, these murals featured harmonious compositions combining flora and fauna. Like the splendid mosaic representing the under-water world in the House of the Faun, such scenes constitute a fabulous catalogue of the various species of birds and types of plant life that were to be found around the villas in the region. This was a clear expression of the wish to capture the surrounding natural world and to bring it into the more intimate confines of the home, the better to immerse oneself in its teeming vigour and to forget one's cares. In the scenes depicted by the painters, nature is represented untrammelled: the birds are not caged, plant life proliferates in joyful confusion. This new type of painting continues the trompe l'oeil tradition of the Second Style; the painstakingly observant description of animal and plant life verges on a dreamy sort of abstraction, reflecting an intense desire to capture an idealized and imaginary reality which, although clothed in the idiom of concrete appearance, did not exist. Here, once again, art and mind are combined in a dream-like approach.

The Third Style seems to be a faithful reflection of Roman society during the First Imperial Period, in all its complexity and local variation. With the easing of political tensions and strife, the tormented compositions of the Second Style fade away and are replaced by a new taste seeking formal balance, simplicity – sometimes even austerity – and a return to the values of the classical world of the past.

A new period of stability was ushered into a world governed by the firmly established system of Roman imperial power, and this taste for order and moderation is reflected in the murals painted during this period. Guided by henceforth unquestionably established principles, artistic imagination and the new-found tranquility of contemporary minds could at last give free rein to their authenticity and express their joy of life.

Garden scene

Detail. Fresco in the Fourth Style. South wall of the garden in the House of the Venus, Pompeii.

The wall which separated the garden from the outside world was decorated with a depiction of Venus shown as an ordinary lower-class woman languorously reclining in a seashell. On either side are magnificent scenes of garden life, such as this elegant long-beaked bird gingerly advancing through luxurious vegetation in a garden enclosed by a wattle fence.

Above

The Three Graces

Fresco in the Third Style.
57 x 53 cm. (22 x 21 in.).
House IX, 2, 16, Pompeii.
Naples, Museo Archeologico
Nazionale.

Opposite

The Three Graces

Fresco in the Third Style.
53 x 47 cm. (21 x 18 in.).
Region VI, *insula occidentalis*, Pompeii.
Naples, Museo Archeologico
Nazionale.

THREE DECADES
OF CHANGE

Mars and Venus
Fresco in the Third Style.
154 x 117 cm. (61 x 46 in.).
House of the Fatal Love, Pompeii.
Naples, Museo Archeologico
Nazionale.

Writing about Nero and his new imperial residence, Suetonius tells us that he "built a palace that stretched from the Palatine to the Esquiline Hill. It was so spacious that it accommodated a triple colonnade one mile long, and a lake as large as the sea, surrounded by scores of buildings, as numerous as in a city. All around were vast expanses of greenery, fields, pastures, vineyards and woods filled with wild animals." The *Domus Aurea*, the most fabulous residence ever recorded in human history, at any place or in any time, can be seen as more than just the creation of an omnipotent Roman emperor giving free rein to his extravagant fancy. It also mirrored the mood and tastes of a society which, after having experienced the austerity and rigours of the Augustan era, was bent on indulging in every voluptuous excess. In all of the cultural manifestations of this period is to be sensed an almost obsessive desire to astonish and to amaze, to adopt a lifestyle in which extremes become the daily reality. Licence became the rule in all areas; life seems to have turned into a mere pretext for the most unbridled pleasures. The fate of the gladiators in the arena depended upon the whims of the crowd; Christian prisoners were burned alive to serve as torches. The emperor Claudius ordered one hundred ships – including huge triremes and quadriremes – to be transported to the Lake of Fucino in the Apennine mountains to stage a naval battle which

featured a cast of nineteen thousand and ended up in a veritable bloodbath. Nero had Sporus castrated so that he could marry him, while, in a definitely more mundane vein, buyers vied every day to find the biggest and most unusual fish in the market in order to impress guests at the next banquet. Such was the temper of an age, teeming with such "baroque" manifestations.

These excesses and eccentricities invariably found expression in the realm of art. The austere and elegant residence built by Augustus on the Palatine Hill was replaced by the outrageous luxury of Nero's *Domus Aurea*. In painting, the decorative simplicity of the Third Style was gradually replaced by an exuberance, a taste for the baroque and the spectacular which had emerged under the reign of Claudius, and which was to undoubtedly find its most unbridled expression in the murals painted by Fabullus for Nero's palace.

PICTORIAL DECORATION: THE FOURTH STYLE

In its later phase, the Third Style had manifested a tendency to overload the wall surface with decorations of all kinds. The *aediculae*, or central framing elements of the figurative scenes, had progressively disintegrated to become mere ornamental panels in which representations of architecture were again used to create the effects of openings or spatial depth, while curved and undulating linear elements – which gave the illusion of concave and convex spaces – tended to fill the entire pictorial surface. Autonomous representations of "miniaturized" architecture were still depicted in the upper zones, but these were given ever more complicated perspective effects in which an accumulation of figurative motifs – small tableaux, half-open doors, masks, tripods, and *oscilla* – were mingled with an ever-diminishing regard to thematic coherence or pictorial unity. One of the most telling examples of this style can be seen in the house of Marcus Lucretius Fronto (V, 4, a): the murals there display an endless profusion of polychrome floral motifs, while the borders of the lateral panels are brimming with minutely-rendered details and Apollonian and Dionysian symbols.

Such tendencies became even more accentuated in the Fourth Style. The lateral panels of the central zones of the wall often "opened up", affording glimpses of architectural perspectives

Mars and Venus
Details.

133

Above

Centaur and Maenad

Detail. Fresco in the Third Style.
30 x 136 cm. (12 x 54 in.).
Villa of Cicero, Pompeii.
Naples, Museo Archeologico
Nazionale.

Opposite

**Dionysus as a child
riding a panther**

Mosaic in the First Style.
163 x 163 cm. (64 x 64 in.).
House of the Faun, Pompeii.
Naples, Museo Archeologico
Nazionale.

which projected the gaze beyond the wall surface. In some instances, the entire wall has been given over to fantastic and complex architectural forms that are a far cry from the "realistic" depictions of the Second Style. The colours themselves became harsh and strident and the former harmonious alternation between two background colours now exploded in violent tonal contrasts. Painstakingly miniaturized ornamental designs, rendered with a near-obsessive precision, literally swamped the walls in a mingled confusion and in an apparent proclamation of *horror vacui*. The composition of the panels at times resembled a carpet, stretched out like a tapestry; at others, it seemed to wave and flutter in the breeze, as in the example to be seen in the House of the Old Hunt (VII, 4, 48), where the borders of the murals provide the painters with an opportunity to display their virtuosity in a profusion of decorative effects. The eye is eventually drawn to the centre of the panel with its various figures – flying or inscribed in medallions – and its genre scenes and landscapes. The new manner in which these scenes are painted, however, is in total contradiction with the overloaded borders of the pictorial "carpets" that characterized this style. The flowing line and "impressionistic" brushwork, and the judicious use of cast shadows to add volume to the bodies of the figures, tend to create a very lifelike feeling. Similarly, in the landscapes in particular, the alternation of light and dark brushstrokes creates chiaroscuro effects and a sensation of depth.

Although extremely varied, these tendencies were expressed within the framework of very clearly established canons and compositional principles. Thus, in humbler dwellings, one often finds examples of less elaborate and less costly murals. In these cases, complex ornamentation has been rejected in favour of a simple arrangement of variously coloured panels enhanced with small pictures featuring endlessly repeated, hackneyed motifs that draw on "models" from the traditional Greek repertoire.

THE PARADEISOI, OR PAINTED MENAGERIES

Along with such decorative cycles, many houses also possessed vast figurative murals – mythological scenes like the birth of Venus, hunting scenes where wild beasts are depicted fighting in the midst of surrealistic landscapes – taking up the entire surface of the panel

Satyr and Maenad
Fresco in the Fourth Style.
44 x 37 cm. (17 x 15 in.).
House of the Epigrams, Pompeii.
Naples, Museo Archeologico
Nazionale.

Sleeping Maenad

Fresco in the Third Style.
230 x 153 cm. (91 x 60 in.).
House of the Citharist, Pompeii.
Naples, Museo Archeologico
Nazionale.

A maenad sleeps soundly after having
exhausted herself in orgiastic dance.
Her tambourine and thyrsus have
slipped from her hands. Dionysusis
about to join her.

or, at times, the entire rear wall of the garden. These spectacular compositions apparently attempt to emulate the incredible splendour of Oriental seraglios or *paradeisoi*, the vast private parks in which wild animals were left free to roam. In some instances, as in the House of Orpheus (VI, 14, 20), a mythological subject was artfully combined with a naturalistic scene: in this case, Orpheus is shown taming animals with the sound of his lyre. On the estates of the wealthiest Romans it was not rare to see parks with uncaged, wild animals. The writer Varro tells us that, long before Nero, a certain Hortensius created a veritable zoological park near Ostia and entertained his guests by having a slave, disguised as Orpheus, calm the animals with music and song. Here, once again, pictorial decoration has become a dream-procuring instrument; visual pleasures compensate agreeably for those vainly promised by an ardently sought, yet inaccessible, material wealth.

POPULAR PAINTING

The art of this period was by no means limited to such elaborate and sophisticated productions. Painting of a more popular inspiration was a completely independent art-form with a tradition of its own, and many examples have come down to us. Unschooled in the pictorial codes derived from Greek art, the popular or folk painters represented scenes of everyday life with a masterful blend of simplicity and spontaneity. Their paintings were generally executed for shop signs or shrines for the family deities, or *Lares*. These small pictures represent genre scenes of tavern life, craftsmen and merchants at work, religious processions, bustling crowds at the forum, and even explicit scenes of sexual play: in short, the full range of human activities and social events. The narrative style of such paintings make them valuable historical documents of everyday life in ancient times; this is also the case with the bas-reliefs of similar popular origin which display a unique freshness of inspiration and lively handling comparable at times to that of the comic strip.

As in certain sculpted bas-reliefs of this period, this painting genre could be used to capture some current event – almost as if in a snapshot – such as the famous little picture depicting the memorable fight that broke out in the amphitheatre between the Pompeians and the Nocerans in 59 A.D.

Above

Theseus and the Minotaur

Mosaic in the Second Style.
Diam. 45 cm. (18 in.).
Pompeii.
Naples, Museo Archeologico
Nazionale.

Opposite

Theseus, the liberator

Fresco in the Fourth Style.
97 x 88 cm. (38 x 35 in.).
House of Gaius Rufus, Pompeii.
Naples, Museo Archeologico
Nazionale.

Having slain the Minotaur, who lies
on the ground at the entrance to the
labyrinth, Theseus is acclaimed by the
young Athenians before the astounded
Cretans.

Ariadne

Fresco in the Fourth Style.
76 x 70 cm. (30 x 28 in.).
House of Meleager, Pompeii.
Naples, Museo Archeologico Nazionale.

MOSAICS AND STUCCOES

The baroque taste of the Fourth Style also found expression in the decoration of floors and pavements. Complicated figurative compositions made up of black and white tesserae, usually found in the entrances of the houses, proudly proclaim the owner's status. The extremely famous mosaic depicting a watchdog with the caption "*Cave canem*" ("beware of the dog") in the vestibule of the House of the Tragic Poet (VI, 8, 3) is quite typical of this period. Another characteristic example is the mosaic representing a "wounded bear" in the entrance of the eponymous house (VII, 2, 45), where a few coloured tesserae have been incorporated into the overall black and white composition in order to highlight certain parts of the design. The mosaicist attempted to give these figures a luminous touch – echoing a fashionable trend in contemporary painting – by using white tesserae not only for the contours, but also in certain details of the otherwise all-black animal, like white brushstrokes suggesting volume.

At the same time, a new interest in stucco decoration emerged. This was employed in combination with painted wall decoration, as in the tablinum of the House of Meleager (VI, 9, 2). Above all, however, it was used for the cornices running along the walls at ceiling height. Initially smooth and light in tone, these were now punctuated with palmette and brightly-coloured lotus bloom designs. Public buildings, and also the thermae, provide ample evidence of a revived taste for the decorative manner of the First and Second styles which the Third Style, indifferent to relief effects, had tended to neglect. Entire walls, like those of the gymnasium in the baths of Stabiae, and ceilings were decorated with stucco. Because of its rich colouring, its capacity to evoke movement through three-dimensional motifs, its vast figurative repertoire, and the difficuly of execution which placed such ornamention beyond the financial means of most, stucco decoration is one of the most significant aspects of the artistic production of this period.

With its extraordinary variety and originality, the Fourth Style appears above all as just one expression of a bustling, ostentatious society whose more upwardly-mobile members are aspiring confusedly, and by all available means, to claim their place in the sun.

Hercules finds his son in Arcadia
Detail showing Telephus being suckled by a doe.
Fresco in the Fourth Style.
218 x 182 cm. (86 x 72 in.).
Basilica, Herculaneum.
Naples, Museo Archeologico Nazionale.

EMANCIPATED SLAVES AND NEW ENTREPRENEURS

Emancipated slaves, those who had succeeded in obtaining their freedom, formed a class of "new men" who, starting out from nothing, had by their own efforts alone managed to amass considerable fortunes. They actively sought to acquire social respectability and to assert their new status, both for themselves and for their descendants.

These emancipated slaves, many of whom were of foreign extraction, constituted a new social component which upset the existing balance in the lower classes. Unfettered by traditional family constraints or considerations of rank, and abetted by the economic opportunities of the times, they were unscrupulous in their pursuit of wealth. Once they had achieved their goal, they could quite legitimately aspire to an honourable place in the social hierarchy. Consequently, they strove to surround themselves with an aura of prestige in order to acquire the respectability which money alone could not buy.

Energetic entrepreneurs, skilled in business and commerce, these men represented the dynamic element in Roman society. Whereas the wealth of the traditional aristocracy consisted mainly of real estate and property, the freemen disposed of considerable liquid assets. This accessible capital enabled them to seize immediately market opportunities, or to undertake risky but potentially extremely profitable ventures. Usurious money-lending and the financing of manufacturing projects were the preferred areas in which they operated.

THE EARTHQUAKE OF 62 AND REAL ESTATE SPECULATION

Such phenomena, fairly widespread throughout the Roman world, reached a particularly high pitch in Pompeii after the violent earthquake of 62 A.D. which caused considerable damage provided ample opportunities for rebuilding work. With such huge amounts of liquid capital at their disposal, many of these "nouveau-riche" entrepreneurs found themselves ideally placed to engage in profitable ventures, essentially involving real-estate speculation. Splendid properties changed hands. The entrepreneurs took

advantage of the fact that old wealthy Roman families now saw little interest in maintaining their expensive villas in the midst of a disaster-stricken environment; at the same time they could easily lay hands on heavily damaged town houses in Pompeii whose owners lacked the funds to undertake the necessary repair work. The ensuing free-for-all was further fuelled by the administrative chaos resulting from the earthquake – there was ample scope for abuse, and for unauthorized and uncontrolled rebuilding. The municipal authorities, themselves involved in an affair involving bribery and corruption, were neither able nor very motivated to exercise their powers and crack down on the offenders.

REDESIGNING THE HOUSES

The signs of a rapid social transformation, essentially an acceleration of the changes already underway in the previous period, are clearly to be seen in many of the surviving houses. The damage caused by the earthquake was hastily repaired, all too often employing make-shift materials and solutions. Bricks were used systematically, irrespective of the original materials, as well as cheap light wooden frameworks. On the more positive side, this calamity gave members of the various social and economic classes an excellent opportunity to radically redesign or alter the structure of their homes.

The House of Menander, which belonged to one of the noblest families of Pompeii – the one into which Poppaea Sabina, Nero's wife, was born – was redesigned with an evident eye to real estate speculation: the ceilings of the rooms to the right of the atrium were lowered to permit the construction of an upper story. Certain houses with direct access to the street via outside stairs were turned into bordellos – run, naturally, by the servants. To enlarge the House of the Ephebe, several existing adjacent houses were joined together. Upper stories were built wherever feasible. In order to add a series of rooms above the tablinum in the House of the Caeii (I, 6, 15), the owners did not shrink from covering the frescoes in the atrium by constructing a wooden staircase.

Even in those houses which seem not to have undergone alterations, a change in the inhabitants' social staus can be

Achilles on Skyros
Fresco in the Fourth Style.
140 x 90 cm. (55 x 35 in.).
House of the Dioscuri, Pompeii.
Naples, Museo Archeologico
Nazionale.

Achilles and Cheiron

Fresco in the Fourth Style.
125 x 127 cm. (49 x 50 in.).
Basilica, Herculaneum.
Naples, Museo Archeologico
Nazionale.

The Sacrifice of Iphigenia

Fresco in the Fourth Style.
140 x 138 cm. (55 x 54 in.).
Peristyle of the House of the Tragic
Poet, Pompeii.
Naples, Museo Archeologico
Nazionale.

This mural features simultaneous
representations of several episodes
in the myth of Iphigenia, the daughter
of Agammemnon, who was sacrificed
to ensure victory in the military
expedition against Troy.
The young woman, forcibly carried off
by Ulysses and Diomedes, is in the
centre of the composition.
Her grieving father covers his head
with his cloak, while Calcantus,
the priest, hesitates. In the sky,
Artemis is shown welcoming the
young woman riding on the back of
a deer sent by the goddess to save her.

observed. Impressive old houses with atriums from the Samnite Period were thoroughly converted and turned into apartments for rental. To cite only a few examples: in the House of Ariadne (VII, 4, 31/51), the rooms surrounding the second peristyle were redesigned to install a laundry and workshops for the transformation of agricultural produce; in the nearby House of the Sculptured Capitals, a loom was installed in the peristyle, while various textile workshops were set up in the House of the Colonnade Cenaculum (VI, 12, 1-5) and in the house at VI, 13, 6; Sallustus' austere dwelling was coverted into an inn, a restaurant was installed in the House of the Bear, while the house at V, 1, 15 was converted into a bordello.

The housing crisis caused by the earthquake was compounded by the arrival in the city of craftsmen flocking in to meet the urgent demand for rebuilding and conversion work. The resulting scarcity of accommodation was relieved to some extent by a spectacular increase in the number of inns. There were forty-four inns in Pompeii alone, a considerable number for a city that probably had no more than twelve thousand inhabitants.

Small painted advertisements have been found on the façades of houses that had been coverted for multiple occupation. On the block that includes the House of Pansa (VI, 6), one of the oldest dwellings from the Samnite Period, can be see a sign which reads "As from the first of July, in this block of buildings, formerly belonging to Arrius Pollio and now owned by Cnaeus Alleius Nigidius Maius, shops with mezzanines, first floor apartments for knights, and other lodgings will be available for rental. Please contact Primus, servant of Cnaeus Alleius Nigidius Maius." In a similar vein, a sign in the block belonging to Julia Felix advertised: "For rent in the property of Julia Felix, daughter of Spurius, baths frequented by a select society, shops, mezzanines, first-floor apartments, with five-year leases starting on the 13th of August and valid until the sixth year. At the end of the fifth year, the lease is renewable by mutual consent."

Quite modern in its conception, this veritable "complex" combined sections reserved for private lodgings, stores for commercial activities and places for public gatherings – baths, pools and installations for a variety of sports activities such as ball games. The apse of the *calidarium* which had large bay windows overlooking a garden – like the suburban thermae – showed that

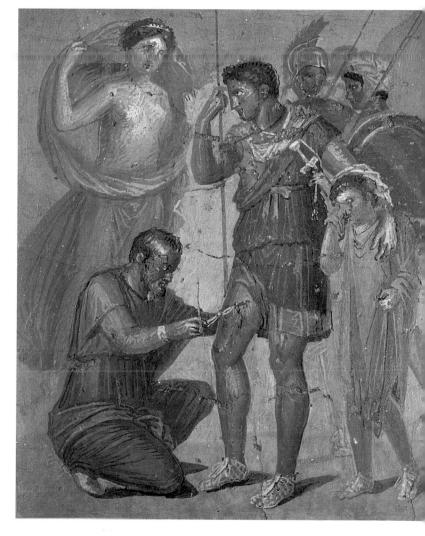

Æneas wounded
Fresco in the Fourth Style.
45 x 48 cm. (18 x 19 in.).
House of Siricus, Pompeii.
Naples, Museo Archeologico Nazionale.

The wounded Æneas puts his arm around his weeping son, Ascanius, while Iapyx, the surgeon, extracts the arrow from his wound. In the foreground, two Trojan warriors and Venus rush to protect Æneas. The Trojan War was one of the most frequent subjects of the Pompeian murals.

Roman architecture had by then completely subordinated the quality of housing to that of the environment and the esthetic values of the landscape. These large expanses of glass installed in the baths, where a high temperature had to be maintained, had the obvious drawback of causing a considerable loss of heat. But the spectacle of nature in whatever form had become an indispensable feature of city life, and such expenditure was considered a necessary luxury. In the section reserved for private use, a long portico with marble pilasters framed a garden; in the middle of the garden ran a watercourse which could be crossed by small footbridges and had pools large enough to stock fish.

This garden, a veritable open-air temple of Isis, with its fountains, statues (including a terracotta figure of one of the seven legendary sages, Pythacus of Mytilenus) and other decorative features, was designed to offer the cultivated visitor an idyllic setting for religious contemplation. It was located opposite a marble triclinium equipped with a nymphaeum, also faced with marble. Beyond the porticoes of the garden, the view took in a lush landscape. The restaurant proposed a range of menus catering for a varied clientele: in the thermopolium, snacks could be bought for immediate consumption, or meals could be eaten while comfortably seated at stone tables; there were even stone couches available for banquets.

THE SUMMER TRICLINIUM

One of the most noteworthy elements of private architecture at the time was the stone triclinium, which increasingly tended to be installed in gardens and other outdoor settings. Like the nymphaea, the idea was to transpose the comforts and pleasures of the resort villas into urban dwellings. The triclinium, directly inspired from the *stibadium*, a type of outdoor couch widely used in the Hellenistic world and in Alexandria, was readily adopted by Pompeians, who lived in a climate mild enough to permit outdoor activities almost all year round. This outdoor banqueting couch was ideally suited to the luxury of the nymphaeum and was often installed near fountains.

In the magnificent House of the Ephebe, the summer triclinium was installed under a columned pergola and lit at night by the bronze statue of an ephebe holding a torch. Water

Zephyr and Chloris

Fresco in the Fourth Style.
189 x 243 cm. (74 x 96 in.).
House of the Ship, Pompeii.
Naples, Museo Archeologico
Nazionale.

Amazon

Fresco in the Fourth Style.
89 x 79 cm. (35 x 31 in.).
Herculaneum.
Naples, Museo Archeologico
Nazionale.

This painting occupies the upper left
portion of a wall divided into several
pictorial compartments. The trompe-
l'œil effect gives an illusion of an
architectural perspective seen through
a window. On the balustrade sits the
figure of an Amazon armed with a
double-axe and a small Greek shield
called a *pelta*. Compositions with
figures and architecture are often to be
seen in the compartmentalized murals.

from a small artificial waterfall fed by a fountain-statue ran
directly in front of the three couches. Murals of a hunting scene
with wild animals, a series of panels depicting the fertility of the
flooded Nile, and an outdoor banquet scene with an embracing
couple – egged on by the other revellers – completed this
enchanting decor. In the house of Octavius Quartio, the water
from a nymphaeum behind the banquet couch (a model large
enough for two) ran into a canal bordered by Egyptian-inspired
statues and a small temple dedicated to Isis.

In the House of Neptune and Amphitrite at Herculaneum,
the summer triclinium was set in a decor that included a
nymphaeum with a fountain and marble theatre masks. On the
rear wall, a colourful mosaic made of glass tesserae depicted the
water god with his wife, Amphitrite.

The summer triclinium was not only a luxury item intended
for the display of wealth and social rank, it was also an eminently
practical piece of garden furniture which took up little space and
could be installed at relatively little cost. Scores of outdoor
tricliniums with pergolas were installed in the estates adjacent to
the amphitheatre, where much land was still being used for
agricultural purposes: vineyards or fields of flowers for the
perfume industry. In this particular area, even the more ordinary
dwellings – no matter how small, such as houses where craftsmen
lived and worked – were equipped with a triclinium, though in
some cases it seems to have been little more than symbolic. The
appetite of the economic elite for luxury seems to have developed
into a mass phenomenon, and essentially for commercial ends.
These tricliniums could indeed be rented for banquets, and, given
the proximity of the amphitheatre, it was a convenient place to
meet and relax for those who had travelled long distances to
watch the gladiator fights.

THE RISE TO POWER:
POPIDIUS CELSINUS AND JULIUS POLYBIUS

The considerable financial resources commanded by the
nouveaux riches, coupled with their yearning for social
recognition, invariably led them to aspire to political power, the
natural sequel to commercial power. Indeed, in the Roman
world, this was the means to acquiring social prestige, to being

appointed to some official function, and of course to enjoying the privileges that came with it, the rich man being transformed into civic dignitary.

The desire for social success and status was a notable characteristic of Pompeian life during this period. The story of two particular individuals will give a good idea of how this process operated.

Numerius Popidius Ampliatus was a former slave who had originally been born into one of the oldest families of Pompeii. Being emancipated and, more importantly, having accumulated a substantial fortune, he received the highest marks of official recognition: an appointment as *minister* of the Fortuna Augusta. This was one of the highest honours to which one could aspire at the time. Not having been born a freeman, however, he was excluded from the magistrature, from participating in the municipal administration, and from sitting at the council of Decurions, the local senate. On the other hand, his wealth could be put to good use for the benefit of the city. The compromise solution that was devised called for him play the generous role of patron of the arts – with interest. In the name of his son, Numerius Popidius Celsinus, he underwrote the entire cost of restoring the Temple of Isis, which had been completely destroyed by the eartquake of 62. In exchange for his magnanimity, the Senators of Pompeii co-opted his son Celsinus and gave him a seat. The story could end there, were it not for a certain detail that sheds light not only on the anecdote, but also the reasons that motivated wealthy entrepreneurs to seek political office, not to mention the ways and means whereby the ruling class ensured the financing of public works. The fact is that when Celsinus was appointed senator, he was only six years old, and thus totally incapable of exercising the function to which he had been appointed. But by admitting the descendants of Numerus Popidius Ampliatus into the aristocratic circles of Pompeii, with the evident privileges and prestige which this promotion entailed, the municipal council assured itself of having access to his ample resources.

During this period, places among the privileged few holding public office in the city were still highly coveted, even though they generally involved ever greater outlays of personal funds. Within several decades, however, the expenditure increased to such a point that Pliny the Younger, writing to Emperor Trajan,

complained of the difficulty of finding citizens worthy – i.e. wealthy – enough to accept the office of decurion. In a subsequent development, when the decurions became directly responsible for collecting taxes, and even though they had to guarantee the revenues *in toto* with their own assets, the available seats in the local senates were almost immediately snatched up by men with correspondingly huge fortunes, regardless of their status at birth. On the other hand, at the end of the Imperial Period, the most coveted privilege was to belong to the class of the *immunes*, that is, those who were dispensed from taking public office!

But in Pompeii in the late years of the first century A.D., not long before the fatal eruption, it was still considered a privilege to sit in the aristocratic senate. This fact is confirmed by many panels praising the merits of the various candidates, evidence that electoral campaigns were hotly contested even then. These panels also give a record of the complex tactics used by Caius Julius Polybius during his rise to power. His Greek surname is of noble origin and shows that he was the descendant of a slave emancipated by Emperor Augustus who had established himself in Pompeii during the Imperial Period. He owned a splendid house with a double atrium from the Samnite Period which he had purchased in order to live in surroundings worthy of the high social station to which his financial success had raised him. The rich collection of bronze objets d'art found in the house attest to the great luxury enjoyed by its owners. Among the finest of these works of art is the bronze torch-bearing Ephebe in the Archaic style, a large krater decorated with a mythological scene, and a Peloponnesian hydra dating from the Archaic Period, the most valuable piece in a collection of antiquities that was already considered prestigious in its own day.

But Polybius was a "new man" and, although very wealthy, he had had to expend a good deal of effort to further his political career. He seems to have been very active politically under Emperor Vespasian. He eventually consolidated his electorate and so commanded a large body of votes, which he put to good use by making alliances with the "right" people in the municipal government. Demonstrating a keen flair for politics, he put his name and connections at the service of the most influential candidates and supported them unreservedly during their campaigns. His adroit manoeuvering earned him the support he

Triclinium with a fountain

1st cent. A.D.
House of Neptune and Amphitrite,
Herculaneum.

needed when conditions finally proved favourable enough for him to submit his own candidacy.

He had close commercial ties with the bakers' guild and, although careful to cater to his popular electoral base, when he wished to be accepted on an equal footing by the aristocracy he took on the airs of a refined intellectual. On one poster, surely a minor masterpiece of diplomacy, he presents himself as a *studiosus et pistor*, in other words, "scholar and baker." In order to gain favour among large segments of the population, he did not shrink from using his personal fortune for the benefit of the community at large, as well as for certain interest groups in particular, as we can see from this somewhat ambiguous campaign slogan: "Vote for Julius Polybius for the office of aedile. He makes good bread."

TWO PARVENUS: THE VETTII

Aulus Vettius Conviva and Aulus Vettius Restitutus, who were probably closely related, are the two most typical examples of the parvenus who reached eminent positions in Pompeian society. We know very little about these two men, probably both emancipated slaves, but we know their house very well. In fact, it is the house that receives the most visits in Pompeii and it provides a sufficiently eloquent account of their lives and tastes. The House of the Vettii presents a very precise picture of the changes that Pompeian society was undergoing at the time, and allows us to imagine the type of upstarts who arrived on the scene at a fairly late stage. The latter were admirably caricatured by Petronius with his character Trimalcion.

The Vettii were primarily winegrowers and merchants, but they also diversified their activities and benefitted from a variety of other sources of income. The symbolic attributes of their patron divinities, Mercury and Fortuna, are omnipresent in the decor of the house. In the entrance, as a prophylactic measure against the evil eye, or *fascinum*, there is a figure of Priapus with a disproportionately large phallus resting on one side of a set of scales balanced by a purse on the other. On the floor is a mosaic representing a basket full of grapes and other fruits symbolizing the earthly abundance to which the family owed its wealth.

The service entrance of this ancient Samnite house with double atrium was walled up to to allow the construction of small apart-

Opposite

Top

Cupid goldsmiths
Fresco in the Fourth Style.
House of the Vettii, Pompeii.

Bottom

Apollo and Omphala
Detail. Fresco in the Fourth Style.
House of the Vettii, Pompeii.

Overleaf

Imaginary architecture
Coloured stucco in the Fourth Style.
167 x 180 cm. (66 x 71 in.).
House of Meleager, Pompeii.
Naples, Museo Archeologico
Nazionale.

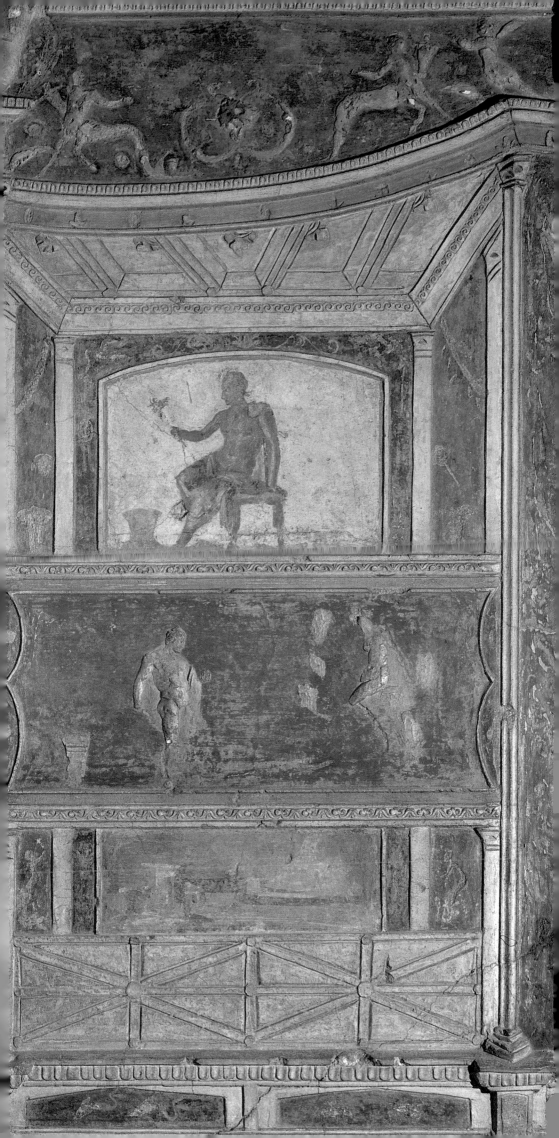

Above

Mars and Venus

Fresco in the Third Style.
253 x 150 cm. (100 x 59 in.).
House of the Citharist, Pompeii.
Naples, Museo Archeologico
Nazionale.

Opposite

Banquet scene with a courtesan

Fresco in the Fourth Style.
59 x 53 cm. (23 x 21 in.).
Herculaneum.
Naples, Museo Archeologico
Nazionale.

ments for rental on the upper story. A small room near the kitchen was used for prostitution by a Greek slave born in the house, Euthichida, who offered her services for a nominal sum. Graffiti inscriptions at the entrance boast of the young woman's charms and professional tariff. Although the Vettii did their best to affect an image of refinement and culture, any small gain, wherever it came from, was not something to be looked down upon.

It was a tradition from Hellenistic times in Pompeii to display portraits of the owners in the atrium, as if symbolically greeting their guests and visitors. Examples of these painted likenesses may be seen in many houses, such as the aristocratic residence from the Samnite Period which is supposed to have belonged to Paquius Proculus, a magistrate belonging to the old Pompeian aristocracy. The double-portrait depicts the master of the house

Amorous prelude

Fresco in the Fourth Style.
31 x 31 cm. (12 x 12 in.).
House of Meleager, Pompeii.
Naples, Museo Archeologico
Nazionale.

and his spouse: he is shown holding a papyrus scroll in the right hand, while she wields a stylus and wax tablet. The message is clear: the owners wished to project an image of themselves as cultivated literate people.

The Vettii had themselves represented in the atrium of their house wearing laurel wreaths, as if they were writers and poets. However, like Trimalcion, they were probably more proficient at keeping track of numbers than at tracing letters. In a highly pedantic and pompous vein, the entire decorative scheme was designed to add a noble veneer to a fortune accumulated in the wine trade. The figurative scenes are peppered with learned and edifying mythological episodes, figures of heroes and muses, portraits of poets and various other real personages. In the same way, Trimalcion, having invited distinguished writers to his table, brazenly ventures to give his opinion on the poets and orators of the day, boasts about having two libraries, one filled with works in Greek the other in Latin, and declares that culture should never be neglected, not even at the dinner table. He then proceeds to cite all sorts of myths and mythological characters completely out of context. Seeing the many murals in the Vettii House, with their complicated programmes of mythological and tragic scenes, it is easy to imagine the Vettii candidly proferring erroneous explanations of them to their guests, and to think immediately of Petronius' character.

The analogy takes on its full sense in the triclinium. It was not enough to flaunt one's culture; it also had to be made clear to the guests that without a certain amount of money, none of this would ever have been possible. Here we can see a charming painted frieze graced with cupids and depictions of the various commercial activities which enabled the owners to fill their coffers and provide such lavish fare. The space devoted to each of the activities was proportional to the importance of the gain procured. Finally, in order to leave no doubt, two money-chests were proudly displayed right in the middle of the atrium; although these stood on legs, the bottom of each chest rested on a stone base so as to prevent collapse under the weight of the contents.

Trimalcion was not only a lifelike portrayal of people such as the Vettii but also the embodiment of the vulgar mentality of a highly successful class in Pompeii, not so different from the one described by Petronius in his satire.

Satyr and Hermaphrodite

Fresco in the Third Style.
51 x 56 cm. (20 x 22 in.).
Pompeii.
Naples, Museo Archeologico
Nazionale.

Erotic scene

Fresco. 1st cent. A.D.
41 x 41 cm. (16 x 16 in.).
Pompeii.
Naples, Museo Archeologico
Nazionale.

IMAGES
OF EVERYDAY LIFE

The outstanding wealth of information yielded by the unique site of Pompeii provides us with a detailed picture not just of the city's history, but above all of the everyday life of its inhabitants. Walking through the streets and houses, it seems as if they want to shake themselves out of a two thousand-year long slumber and talk to us directly about their lives, their hopes, their aspirations, their pleasures and pains. What has come to light from under the layers of ash and lapilli is not just the ruins of ancient monuments, but the content of human lives whose ways and customs may have been different from our own, but which are close to us because of our common humanity. In order to understand and share their joys and suffering, we need only turn to the many vestiges of those bygone days lived two thousand years ago in the protective and menacing shadow of Vesuvius.

RELIGION, MAGIC
AND SUPERSTITION

Established religion in the Roman world had an essentially formal and public function, involving considerations of a political rather than of a personal nature. It was a matter of social rituals celebrated according to set rules, accompanied by unchanging practices and gestures which had to be scrupulously performed in

Above

Temple of Isis

1st cent. A.D.
Pompeii.

Opposite

Ritual celebrating the cult of Isis

Fresco in the Fourth Style.
80 x 85 cm. (31 x 33 in.).
Herculaneum.
Naples, Museo Archeologico
Nazionale.

order to guarantee their effectiveness. Prayer was limited to the formulation of a wish, and the sacrificial offering was a transaction conducted with the divinity under clearly defined circumstances. The cults of the Capitoline triad and of the reigning emperor took on an eminently political character that ensured spiritual cohesion between the many provinces and cities making up the Roman world.

However, the development of philosophical thought had made the more cultivated classes fully aware of the deception and trickery involved in the cult of the Olympian pantheon. Not surprisingly therefore, we see the literate members of the population increasingly turning to cults of Oriental origin, like those of Sabazio, Dionysus and the Great Mother. The cult of Isis became very popular in Pompeii and co-existed alongside those of Venus Fiscia, patron-goddess of the city and avatar of an ancient Italic goddess of the natural life force, Mercury, the god of commerce and communication, and Dionysus-Bacchus, the god of wine and ecstasy. The cult of the Egyptian goddess, which had been imported to Campania via its commercial relations with Alexandria, was adopted by individuals who were attracted to initiatory rituals, or in search of inner peace and eternal bliss in the afterlife. In some of the wealthier homes in Pompeii, we can still see small temples and chapels devoted to Isis and to the powerful *Isiaci* brotherhood. Significantly enough, the Temple of Isis built not far from the triangular forum which was the only public monument to have been completely restored after the earthquake of 62.

The splendid Villa of the Mysteries, with its huge murals depicting Dionysian themes, provides us, via the allegories of artistic language, with much information about this particular cult. In fact, during the Republican Period, the observance of, and initiation into the Dionysian mysteries had been forbidden, although they continued to be celebrated, mostly within the privacy of aristocratic homes.

The cult of family ancestors was observed by all. The *pater familias* was the custodian of this tradition and officiated during the ceremonies. The spirits of the ancestors, or *Lares*, and the guardians of familial harmony, the *Penates*, were worshipped along with the family *genius*, the vital spirit of the family, which was represented in the form of a snake. In each house, there was a small shrine containing figures and statuettes of the tutelary deities of the

Opposite

Citharist
Fresco in the Third Style.
56 x 60.5 cm. (22 x 24 in.).
Pompeii.
Naples, Museo Archeologico
Nazionale.

Below

**The daughters of Leucippos
playing knuckles**
Painting on marble by Alexandros
of Athens. Early 1st cent. A.D.
42 x 89 cm. (17 x 35 in.).
Herculaneum.
Naples, Museo Archeologico
Nazionale.

family. Ritual offerings and libations were cast on a sacred fire before meals. The entire family assembled around the shrine to celebrate important events like marriages, births and deaths.

Superstition had perhaps an even stronger hold on people than religion, especially among the poorer segments of the population. Belief in the malefic influence of the evil eye and envious gaze, or *fascinum*, was widespread and shared by all social classes; the well-to-do were constantly in search of effective means to ward off its effects, or to divert them towards another victim. The *oscilla*, marble masks designed to protect homes from the evil eye, were hung between the columns of the peristyle, as can be seen in the House of the Gilded Amorini. Medallions called *bullae*, often made of gold, were hung around the necks of the children. The phallus, usually carved in the round and placed in the entrances of houses and shops, was the favourite protective charm of the lower classes because it represented the original forces of nature in their positive aspect, and was credited with having the power to neutralize harmful influences. Some houses were placed under the protection of Hercules, the "nice god" or god of Happiness.

Special pots have been unearthed with evidence that the Pompeians had recourse to magical practices such as concocting philters and potions. Another popular procedure was the burial of *defixiones*, slats of wood pierced by a nail and inscribed with the name of the person whom one wished dispatched to Hades.

ELECTORAL PROPAGANDA

Each year in the month of March, debates and tempers flared throughout the city as candidates vied for election to the municipal magistrature. After the senate had assured itself that they did indeed possess the requisite financial means for eligibility, the candidates presented themselves before the assembled populace in the forum and declaimed their political programmes from the orator's tribune, or *suggestum* (traditionally, they sported an immaculate white (*candida*) toga symbolizing the transparency of their lives, hence our English words "candid" and "candidate"). Each year, two new duumvirs and two aediles had to be elected; the first combined the functions of mayor, treasurer and judge, while the latter administered the municipal finances.

Musicians

Details. Mosaic in the First Style
by Dioscurides of Samos.
43 x 41 cm. (17 x 16 in.).
Villa of Cicero, Pompeii.
Naples, Museo Archeologico
Nazionale.

Actor-king

Fresco in the Third Style.
39 x 39 cm. (15 x 15 in.).
Herculaneum.
Naples, Museo Archeologico
Nazionale.

Opposite

**Comedy scene: consulting
a magician**

Mosaic in the First Style.
42 x 35 cm. (17 x 14 in.).
Villa of Cicero, Pompeii.
Naples, Museo Archeologico
Nazionale.

**Bread, walnuts and olives
preserved by ash
from the eruption of Vesuvius**
79 A.D.
Pompeii.
Naples, Museo Archeologico
Nazionale.

Only free male citizens who had reached majority were allowed to vote, but the entire active population, including women and slaves, participated in the process, voicing their support for the candidates. No holds were barred, and the walls of the city were covered with posters, some of them produced on the initiative of ordinary citizens who stated their preferences in cases where two candidates for the same office formed a pre-electoral coalition and presented a common programme. The candidates and their supporters indeed relied on this type of private initiative to drum up potential votes, and also did their best to persuade the electorate by using standard arguments, such as a reminder of results successfully obtained and promises of even better things in store.

The posters generally praised the staunch moral character of the budding magistrates or proclaimed their diverse merits and achievements. There were also instances of counterpublicity, like the tracts posted by inhabitants of the forum district expressing their opposition to the election of a certain Cerrinius Vatia. On such posters, political adversaries and their partisans were openly discredited and variously vilified as "dreamers," "chicken thieves," "renegade slaves," "whoremongers," and even "murderers". Nor did the dissenters shrink from character assassination; couched in subtle irony, one particular verse inscription denounced Paquius Proculus as a homosexual and exhibitionist, and, although he had been elected on a broad consensus, took him to task for disregarding his constituents: "The bleating sheep have elected Proculus aedile. Yet this office required the dignity of an honest man and respect for the function."

The elected officials had to contribute funds out of their own pockets to finance a public building project or hold public games, and of course pay the bureaucrats without whom the city administration could not be run. In return, after a one-year mandate, they were elected life members of the order of decurions, that is, to a place in the municipal senate, the effective seat of power where important debates were held and administrative affairs controlled. By virtue of their rank, the magistrates enjoyed special privileges of a formal and material nature: their houses were supplied with water free of charge, they were entitled to a larger share of any gratuities, and the best seats at the theatre were reserved for them. A final prerogative was that of immunity from being condemned to demeaning penalties.

Bread vendor

Fresco. 1st cent. A.D.
62 x 53 cm. (24 x 21 in.).
House of the Baker, Pompeii.
Naples, Museo Archeologico
Nazionale.

GAMES AND SPECTACLES

The large number of poor and not-so-well-off people in the city obliged the magistrates to find various safety valves to channel or defuse potential social tension. Public games and spectacles were specifically intended to meet this requirement. As we have already mentioned, the magistrates had to finance public works or games, and this in itself is an indication that the latter were considered necessary for the common good. Funerary inscriptions in the tombs of certain Pompeian notables make express mention of the magnificence of the games they subsidized. Many graffiti express enthusiastic gratitude to those who organized the gladiator fights. Not infrequently, one can find small silhouettes of gladiators with their names, victorious exploits and the results of combats, not unlike an illustrated sports chronicle. Many advertisements for public events at the amphitheatre have also been found in Pompeii and in neighbouring towns, suggesting that the athletes had their own supporters who followed them from engagement to engagement, cheering on their favourites. These advertisements mentioned the names of the gladiators about to meet in the arena, and other events such as fights with wild animals, taking care to add that a canvas tarpaulin would be slung over the *cavea* to protect the distinguished spectators from the sun. The gladiators were adulated by their public, and especially by their female admirers; graffiti have been found that boast of their feats not just in the arena, but also in more tender bouts.

Theatre actors, especially pantomimes, also became veritable stars. Apart from graffiti on the walls in Pompeii recording the names of various popular actors and singers, generally emancipated slaves, are to be seen also those inscribed by the "Paridiani", fans of the actor and stage idol Paride. The Roman propensity for order and formality probably explains why there was a law requiring theatres to keep detailed lists of seating arrangements, so that seats could be correctly allotted according to the social rank of each spectator. The right to sit in the *proedria* was an especially prized privilege which was enjoyed *de jure* by the decurions, but could also be obtained by official decree, or in other words for a correspondingly high sum of money – which not a few were more than willing to disburse. Such privileges were one form of

Flour mills

1st cent. A.D.
Bakery of Popidius Priscus, Pompeii.

The hourglass-shaped millstones,
which were made of basalt from
Roccamonfina, were fitted over a fixed
conical bases. The grain was poured in
from the top and crushed
by the grinding action of the stones,
coming out as flour at the bottom.

Still life with a fruit bowl

Detail. Fresco in the Fourth Style.
74 x 234 cm. (29 x 92 in.).
House of Julia Felix, Pompeii.
Naples, Museo Archeologico
Nazionale.

public demonstration and official recognition of the high rank of the individuals who benefitted from them.

Pompeians also enthusiastically followed the games of the *pilicrepi*, or ball players, which took place in the gymnasiums near the baths. Other public diversions were a sort of chess game called *latrunculi*, and games of knuckles or dice, which was the most popular game of chance. One inscription on a wall commemorates the large sums won by a Pompeian from his Noceran opponent. The former announces that he has stooped at nothing to achieve this result, indirectly informing us of the current gaming practices in many of the taverns. Doctored dice loaded with lead have also been found.

FOOD AND DRINK

Full-course meals, "from egg to apple," were served only during banquets held after nightfall in the luxurious torch-lit tricliniums. In between the entrées and desserts, which included all sorts of fruits and cakes, a variety of fish and meat dishes were served. The most popular meats were fowl, beef and pork. Game was also highly appreciated; the woods at the foot of Mt. Vesuvius abounded with hare, pheasant, deer and boar. Meat was generally boiled, grilled or roasted, and almost always garnished with stuffing. In the kitchens of Pompeii, many animal bones have been found, still lying in pots or left in the embers. Meat, which was often spiced, was systematically served with *garum*, a very salty and aromatic condiment obtained by pickling small fish, which were then left to ferment in the sun before being sieved.

Shellfish and other seafood, including the more refined species of fish such as sole and moray eel, were frequent fare on Pompeian tables. Fishing tackle of all kinds was found in warehouses near the harbour. Shellfish, particularly clams and cockles, were commonly eaten as snacks while strolling through gardens, as proved by the many shells found along flower beds in a recent excavation.

One host who often entertained took the precaution of inscribing a series of instructions for his guests on the wall of his triclinium:

"Wash your feet with water, a servant will come and dry them. Cover your place with a towel and take care not to leave any stains on our tablecloth". "Avoid flirting with the wives of others

Still life with rabbit, fruit and birds
Detail. Fresco in the Fourth Style. 41 x 129 cm. (16 x 51 in.). Herculaneum. Naples, Museo Archeologico Nazionale.

or fondling them. See to it that your language is decent and respectful". "Refrain from contradicting your neighbour and abstain from picking arguments. If you can, that is. If not, then leave the table and go home".

Except for banquets, meals were generally frugal and consisted only of a first course and a main dish. Cabbage, onions and garlic were favourite ingredients and widely cultivated in the region. Breakfast was a very simple affair consisting essentially of bread, cheese and leftovers from the previous night's meal. During the day, meals were often eaten outside of the home at the many food-stands that served snacks such as sausages or fried fish. Doughnuts, cookies and cakes, all sweetened with honey, could be bought from street vendors. Lard and vegetable oil were most commonly used in cooking.

There being no tea, coffee or spirits, the only refreshing drink was wine, which was more or less diluted with water according to the time of day. In winter, wine was served mulled, and in summer cooled with snow brought down from the mountains and kept in pits dug into the ground. However, "iceboxes" such as these were a rare luxury. Drinks were commonly sweetened with honey. Sweet wine, "straw wine" or retsina could be bought. Quality varied with the type of vines. Wine from Pompeii, which was an important source of income for the city and widely exported, unfortunately had the reputation of not aging well, and never fetched very high prices.

LOVE, VIRTUE AND VICE

Pompeii was a city dedicated to the goddess Venus, and love in all its forms was practiced and celebrated there. The visible remains of this so-very intimate aspect of social life range from frescoes illustrating the pleasures of the sexual embrace to passionate graffiti furtively inscribed on houses by hopeful lovers to obtain a tryst. Resorting to spontaneous and unsophisticated verse, these street-poets exalted their beloved's charms or despaired over an unrequited love, revealing their innermost feelings to passers-by who could read them and meditate upon them.

Jealousy, that perennial snake in the garden of love, often rears its ugly head in the graffiti. Inscriptions mocked or commiserated with the unfortunate cuckold; in some cases, the latter themselves

Oil lamp

Terracotta. 1st cent. A.D.
Height: 7 cm. (3 in.).
Pompeii.
Naples, Museo Archeologico
Nazionale.

Opposite

Tintinnabulum

Bronze. 1st cent. A.D.
Length: 21 cm. (8 in.).
Herculaneum.
Naples, Museo Archeologico
Nazionale.

The *tintinnabulum* was supposed to
ward off evil spirits by the sound of its
bells. It was hung at the entrances of
houses and shops. The phallus, which
was considered a favourable omen,
was supposed to deflect the evil eye to
other persons.

ruefully pondered a remedy for their affliction. We become privy to such dramas as two men ready to come to blows for the favours of a tavern maid, or the hesitations of virgins or newly-initiated young women, while other, more experienced ladies boldly declare their expectations, proclaim their satisfaction or their disappointment. Even matrons from the best society could not conceal their passion for the more dashing gladiators.

Unbridled sexuality seems to have been the order of the day, and the notion of vice non-existent. Male or female homosexuality was commonly and overtly indulged in; even pedophilia seems to have been regarded as a completely normal sexual practice. Group sessions involving three or more partners were also proposed. At the entrance of specialized establishments, men would taunt the prostitutes. An older man in search of a companion for his later years voices his hope that he will be able to satisfy her. In private homes, male and female slaves were the habitual prey of masters and their guests. Prostitutes working outside the city walls tempted the wayfarers and officiated behind the monuments that lined the road. Others plied their services in bordellos for a paltry sum. Even women from the aristocracy succumbed to the climate of lust and greed while the more cultivated and untouchable beauties haunted the lusty fantasies of rich Pompeians. Men also prostituted themselves; one inscription from a gigolo offer his expert services even to virgins.

With their outspokenly frank graffiti, the walls of Pompeii portray a varied and very real humanity, giving us not just the names of hundreds of individuals, but also a glimpse into their private lives, their love affairs and their misfortunes. As we read the wedding announcements and the messages of the betrothed couple's friends and relatives, we can imagine the wedding processions that once filled the streets, accompanied by the joyful cries of the guests and wellwishers.

But love is also a lasting sentiment, and there are many inscriptions commending the more sober joys of fidelity and moderation, the serene intimacy of life *a due*, like the names found carved side by side above a conjugal bed. This, too, was Pompeii: the uninterrupted pulse of everyday life, the pulse of a heart already two thousand years old, a heart whose fragile and relentless echo continues to resonate, leaving no visitor indifferent.

CONCLUSION

Paquius Proculus and his wife
Fresco in the Fourth Style.
65 x 58 cm. (26 x 23 in.).
House VII, 2, 6, Pompeii.
Naples, Museo Archeologico
Nazionale.

The ruins of ancient Pompeii, discovered in the eighteenth century, continue to exert a strong influence and appeal on Western culture. Writers, poets, painters, graphic artists, photographers, musicians, film-makers and famous travellers visiting the site have been moved by its fate and inspired to recapture its spellbinding atmosphere.

The many relics and vestiges that have been brought to light, the famous "Pompeii red", the decorative grotesques, and the domestic furniture have had a marked influence on modern taste, forming an essential reference point in our evocation of the past. The visitor who strolls through the streets, or enters the houses, shops and workshops of the craftsmen, is struck with amazement at the exuberance of this lost civilization, and not a little melancholy at so stark a demonstration of the precarious and transitory nature of human life.

And yet Pompeii has left us no imposing monuments like the pyramids of Egypt or the temples of Greece, which have so proudly defied the centuries, nor even any particularly outstanding masterpieces of art. The city lying at the foot of mighty Vesuvius reveals to us dwellings of all shapes and sizes, in perpetual transformation, humble shops, and daily objects ranging from the simplest to the most luxurious. But beyond these walls and banal objects we gain direct access to the heart and

Above

Dancing Maenad and Satyr

Polychrome marble inlay.
1st cent. A.D.
23 x 67 cm. (9 x 26 in.).
House VII, 4, 31-51. Pompeii.
Naples, Museo Archeologico
Nazionale.

Opposite

**Architecture with columns
and doorway**

Detail. Fresco in the Second Style.
Central panel.
337 x 169 cm. (133 x 67 in.).
Villa of Fannius Sinistor, Boscoreale.
Naples, Museo Archeologico
Nazionale.

soul of a once-living world and its inhabitants. And Pompeii has perhaps given us something more: the sense of a common humanity perpetually in search of its own identity, struggling with ever the same problems and questions, ever the same hopes and ambitions, and ever the same need for self-assertion throughout its long history.

Pompeii has one interlocutor: man himself. Man of classical antiquity is revealed to our modern understanding in his essence, free of all mystery. Modern man, observing his forbear in the detached universal dimension into which Antiquity, as if by magic, has projected him, has much matter for meditation on his own condition, his own passions and feelings, inevitably influenced by the events of the past. And finally, there is no real difference between these two worlds. The experience of life is the same everywhere and at all times: the shape of the houses and circumstances under which they were built may change, but not the feelings of those who live within their walls.

"There is nothing new under the sun" proclaimed an Old Testament prophet over two thousand years ago. The miracle of the rediscovery of Pompeii has been to enable us to touch the substance of life as it was in Antiquity – and to let it touch us. Inexorably *idem et alius*, similar and different, despite the passage of time. Such is the true message that Pompeii hands down to us, ushering the infinite flow of life into our contemporary awareness.

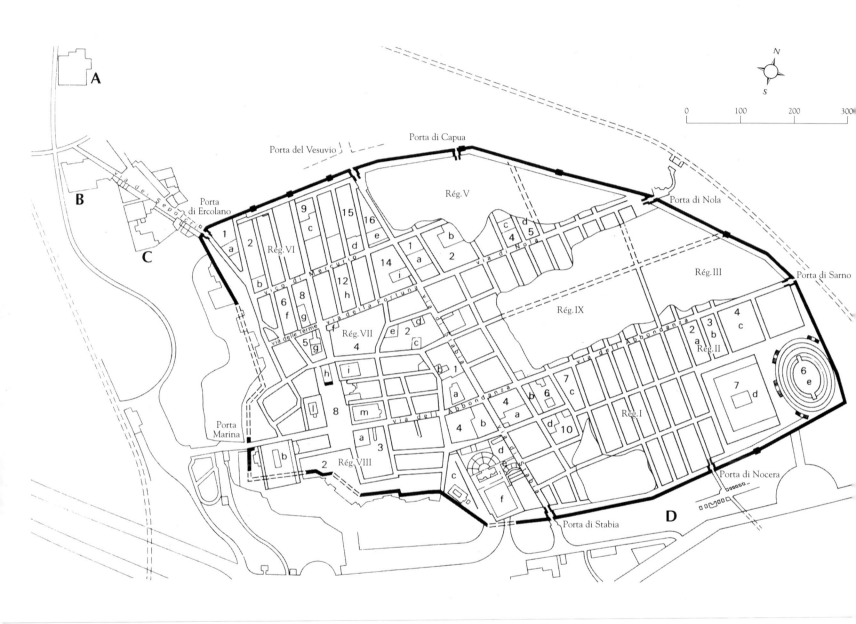

Region I
- 4, a   House of the Citharist
- 6, b   House of the Cryptoporticus
- 7, c   House of Paquius Proculus
- 10, d   House of Menander

Region II
- 2, a   House of Loreius Triburtinus
- 3, b   House of the Venus
- 4, c   House of Julia Felix
- 6, e   Amphitheatre
- 7, d   Palestra

Region V
- 1, a   House of Caecilius Jucundus
- 2, b   House of the Silver Wedding
- 4, c   House of M.L. Fronto
- 5, d   House of the Gladiators

Region VI
- 1, a   House of the Surgeon
- 2, b   House of Sallustus
- 6, f   House of Pansa
- 8, g   House of the Tragic Poet
- 9, c   House of Meleager
- 12, b   House of the Faun
- 14, i   House of Orpheus
- 15, c   House of the Vettii
- 16, e   House of the Gilded Amorini

Region VII
- 1, a   Stabian Baths
- 1, b   Sittius' Inn
- 2, c   House of the Bear
- 2, d   House of Gaius Rufus
- 2, e   Ovens
- 4, f   Temple of Fortuna

- 5, g   Forum Baths
- 8   Forum
- 8, h   Temple of Jupiter
- 8, i   Market (Macellum)
- 8, j   Temple of Apollo
- 8, m   Edifice of Eumachia

Region VIII
- 2, b   Temple of Venus
- 3, a   Comitia
- 4, b   House of Cornelius Rufus
- 4, c   Triangular Forum
- 4, d   Grand Theatre
- 4, e   Odeum
- 4, f   Gladiator Barracks

- A   Villa of the Mysteries
- B   Villa of Diomede
- C   Villa of Cicero
- D   Cemetery

FINDING ONE'S WAY
IN ANCIENT POMPEII

A stranger arriving in the ancient city of Pompeii for the first time would have been able to find his way only by indirect means – by asking other people how to get to wherever he wanted to go.

Adresses of houses were indicated only in summary form and according to very sketchy guidelines, such as the name of a district or the nearest public building.

An inscription on a wall in Pompeii gives the address of a woman in Nocera who had aroused many passions and whose reputation had spread by word of mouth: "In Nocera, ask for Novella Primigenia, near the Roman Gate, in the Venus quarter." This type of formulation obliged visitors to ask neighbours for directions. People lived in much closer contact then, and most knew each other either by name or by sight. It was not so difficult, finally, to find a particular individual or house. As we have already noted, neighbourhood relations were important factors in election campaigns and propaganda, and ties to the local community were both close and strong. Functioning according to unwritten rules strongly rooted in local tradition, they permitted the spontaneous exchange of services, as well as a feeling of security and solidarity.

Vestigial inscriptions tell us the names of two of Pompeii's city gates, the Porta Salina and the Porta Urbulana, as well as of several streets and buildings, and various quarters. These quarters or

Procession with a stretcher
Fresco. 1st cent. A.D.
66 x 75 cm. (26 x 30 in.).
Façade of workshop VI, 7, 8, Pompeii.
Naples, Museo Archeologico
Nazionale.

sections also defined administrative constituencies that played an important role in election campaigns. The names of the quarters were linked to specific locations or features of the city: thus, the *Urbulanenses* lived in the section near the Porta Urbulana (today called Porta Sarno), the *Salinienses* near the Porta Salina (today's Porta Ercolano), the *Campanienses* near the Porta di Capua (renamed Porta di Nola), the *Forenses* near the forum or the Porta Forensa (today's Porta Marina), while the *Pagani* lived in the Pagus Augustus Felix Suburbanus, a suburb beyond the city walls.

In the nineteenth century, in order to facilitate scientific research, Giuseppe Fiorelli subdivided Pompeii into nine sections, or *regiones*, each of which included several *insulae*, or blocks of buildings defined by certain streets (with the exception of the *insula occidentalis*), which were numbered in the order in which they were excavated. The houses located within these blocks were also numbered. In blocks which have not yet been fully excavated, the houses have no numbers, but are indicated by letters of the alphabet. The reference "VII, 4, 48" means that the house is at no. 48 in block 4 of Region VII.

The names given in modern times to the houses and villas only rarely refer to their original occupants (House of the Vettii, House of Lucretius Fronto), who in many cases have not been identified with any certainty. The names refer more often than not to specific discoveries that have been made there (House of the Faun, House of the Ephebe, House of the Indian Statuette, etc.), or to events linked to the time of their discovery (House of the Centenary, House of the Silver Wedding, etc.), to certain architectural or decorative features (House of the Colonnade Cenaculum, House of the Four Styles, etc.), or to pictures and portraits found there (House of Menander, House of Orpheus).

POMPEII:
PROTECTING
A HERITAGE

Pompeii is a living organism, not only because its streets and houses still resonate with the life of the ancient world, but also because, with its rediscovery, it has launched into a new existence. At present, hundreds of people work in Pompeii every day to excavate, restore, maintain and administer the site, which is visited by upwards of a million and a half visitors each year.

Pompeii, however, is also a very fragile, sprawling organism, requiring the attention of many specialists and the application of highly specific techniques.

The city was simply not designed to withstand the centuries. Many of the houses were built with cheap materials and periodically converted as the need arose, while the frescoes were renovated about once in every generation. We have the very difficult and delicate task of preserving these fragile vestiges as long as possible and, no less importantly, without impairing them by removal from their original context.

At the present time, and particularly following the 1980 earthquake which caused serious damage, the work of preservation has clearly taken priority over the work of excavation. And here it is less a matter of restoring and preserving individual buildings, than of saving entire sections of the city, while taking all the other elements – architecture, decor, gardens, etc. – into consideration. The research programme initially involves dwellings in the south-

Scene on the Nile
Fresco in the Fourth Style.
75 x 127 cm. (30 x 50 in.).
Peristyle of House VIII, 5, 24, Pompeii.
Naples, Museo Archeologico
Nazionale.

Scenes of the Nile, a frequent subject
in Pompeian painting, were sometimes
intended as caricatures.

west part of the city. Excavated during the 1950s, and although of capital importance to our understanding of the urban topography as a whole, they have only been partially studied and are not so familiar to the public.

Archaeological investigation today has become veritable laboratory work. Archaeologists must call on the scientific expertise of a host of specialists in order to gain a precise understanding of what they have excavated. Thus small fragments of charcoal are analyzed in order to determine the type of wood used for the roof timbers, or the remains of substances found in the kitchen pots carefully examined to identify what exactly such pots contained. In the gardens, casts are made of the holes left by root systems and traces of pollen are sought to find out what kind of plants were grown and in what order. Human bones are analyzed to learn more about diseases and nutritional habits. Specialists painstakingly reconstruct the remains of animals, study remnants of food and other elements – from the microscopic to the macroscopic (for example, the agricultural landscape along the Sarno River, or the habitat at the foot of Vesuvius) – which were long considered secondary or unimportant. Every possible piece of evidence is scrutinized in order to help us reconstruct the ancient way of life.

With the help of computer technology and accurate research methods, art historians can now study the relationship between the painted decoration on the walls and the mosaics on the floors, or between the choice of pictorial subjects and the function of the rooms in which they were represented. Exact measurements of the rooms and comparisons of their proportions enable the different types of housing to be categorized, while comparative analyses of the materials used for specific purposes help us to establish a detailed model of the socio-economic characteristics of the various classes of Pompeian society and their distribution throughout the various quarters.

Ultimately, to know Pompeii and to understand it in its essence, to analyze its composite elements and to preserve it like a fragile body, to hand down its message in order to perpetuate its existence, is both an act of love and a duty incumbent upon modern man, not only towards his ancestors, but above all towards future generations.

Still life with peaches
Detail. Fresco in the Fourth Style.
33 x 119 cm. (13 x 47 in.).
Pompeii.
Naples, Museo Archeologico
Nazionale.

GLOSSARY

Alae: living-rooms opening onto the atrium on each side of the *tablinum*.

Atriensis: the guardian of the house.

Bulla: an amulet worn by children around the neck.

Calidarium: a heated room for hot baths at the thermae.

Capitolium: temple in Roman cities dedicated to the Capitoline triad: Jupiter, Juno and Minerva.

Cardo: a street which crossed Roman cities along the north-south axis.

Cartibulum: marble table placed near the *impluvium*.

Caupona; an inn.

Cavea: the seating section of an amphitheatre or ancient theatre.

Cella: the temple sanctuary where the cult statue was worshipped.

Cenaculum: small first floor apartment .

Clientes: persons of subordinate rank having dealings with a patrician family.

Compluvium: roof-opening over the atrium to allow rainwater to run into the *impluvium*.

Decurion: member of the municipal senate.

Diaeta: pleasant abode.

Dominus: the master of the house.

Doryphorus: Greek term for a soldier armed with a spear.

Euripe: Greek term designating a small watercourse running through a garden.

Exedra: open air salon with an apse for conversation.

Familia: social unit consisting of all the members of a family and their servants.

Fascinum: evil eye.

Frigidarium: room for cold baths at the thermae.

Genius: a spirit present in each human being, in every thing and place, and even in actions.

Gens: group of persons sharing the same family origins.

Grotesques: fanciful ornamental designs consisting of combinations of figures, volutes and rinceaux.

Gymnasium: a hall for physical training and sports.

Impluvium: basin in the atrium placed underneath the *compluvium* to collect rainwater, which was then channeled to a cistern.

Insula: block of houses.

Lapilli: small porous rocks expulsed by erupting volcanoes.

Lychnophoroi: bronze statues used as torch holders.

Macellum: market.

Magister: official responsible for the administration of a quarter.

Negotiator: merchant, businessman, shipowner.

Negotium: commerce, trade, or political office.

Nymphaeum: room or grotto dedicated to the nymphs; monumental fountain with niches in the form of grottoes.

Oecus: salon or reception room.

Opus vermiculatum: mosaic with figurative motif or geometric designs made of tiny coloured tesserae.

Opus sectile: figurative or geometric decoration usually made up of coloured marble tesserae.

Oscillum: carved marble mask to ward off the *fascinum*; it was hung so that it could be swung in passing.

Otium: any leisure activity: study, meditation, writing, conversation.

Paradeisos: Greek term designating a garden with freely roaming animals.

Parasta: pilaster, or half-column.

Pergula: mezzanine.

Pictor imaginarius: Painter specialized in figurative motifs.

Pilicrepi: ball players.

Protome: carved high or low relief representing the hind parts of animals.

Prodigium: a wonderful and awesome event.

Proedria: lower part of the *cavea* in a theatre, where the notables and wealthy were seated.

Regio: region, or a city district or quarter.

Scutulatum: floor paved with cubic patterns shown in perspective.

Stibadium: open-air *triclinium*.

Suggestum: orator's tribune.

Surges: English word designating high-temperature emanations of volcanic gases.

Taberna: shop opening out on the street with large stalls.

Tablinum: part of the atrium located on the same axis as the entrance.

Tabula picta: easel painting.

Telamon: male figure used as an architectural ornament to support cornices and bays.

Tepidarium: moderately heated room in a bathing establishment which formed a transition between the *calidarium* and *frigidarium*.

Thermopolium: outdoor stand where drinks and snacks were sold.

Triclinium: dining room equipped with couches for eating in a reclining position.

BIBLIOGRAPHY

The classic bibliographic reference on Pompeii is:

H.B. VAN DER POEL, *Corpus topographicum Pompeianum.. Pars IV: Bibliography*, Rome 1977. An updated edition by J. de Waele, with a thematic bibliography by A. Varone, will soon be published.

AA., VV., *La regione sotterrata del Vesuvio. Studi e prospettive*, Naples 1982.

J.P. ADAM, *Dégradation et restauration de l'architecture pompéienne*, Paris 1983.

C. AZIZA, *Le rêve sous les ruines*, Paris 1992.

A. BARBET, *La peinture murale romaine*, Paris 1985.

J.P. DESCŒUDRES (ed.), *Pompeii revisited. The Life and Death of a Roman Town*, Sydney 1994.

W. ERHARDT, *Stilgeschichtliche Untersuchungen an römischen Wandmalereien von der späten Republik bis zur Zeit Neros*, Mainz 1987.

R. ÉTIENNE, *La vie quotidienne à Pompéi*, Paris 1977.

R. ÉTIENNE, *Pompéi, la cité ensevelie*, Paris 1987.

L. FRANCHI DELL'ORTO (ed.), *Ercolano 1738-1988. 250 anni di ricerca archeologica*, Rome 1993.

L. FRANCHI DELL'ORTO and A. VARONE (editors), *Rediscovering Pompeii*, Rome 1990.

E.K. GAZDA (ed.), *Roman Art in the Private Sphere. New Perspectives on the Architecture and Decor of the Domus, Villa and Insula*, Ann Arbor 1991.

P. GRIMAL, *Pompéi, demeures secrètes*, Paris 1992.

R. GUERDAN, *Pompéi, mort d'une ville*, Paris 1973.

W. JONGMAN, *The Economy and Society of Pompeii*, Amsterdam 1988.

E. LA ROCCA, M. and A. DE VOS, *Guida archeologica di Pompei*, Milan 1981.

P. LAURENCE, *Roman Pompeii. Space and Society*, London and New York 1994.

R. LING, *Roman Painting*, Cambridge 1990.

H, MIELSCH, *Die römische Villa: Architektur und Lebensform*, Munich 1987.

L. RICHARDSON Jr., *Pompeii: an architectural History*, Baltimore and London 1988.

K. SCHEFOLD, *La peinture pompéienne. Essai sur l'évolution de sa signification*, Brussels 1972.

A. WALLCE-HADRILL, *Houses and Society in Pompeii and Herculaneum*, Princeton 1994.

P. ZANKER, *Stadtbilder als Spiegel von Gesellschaft und Herrschaftsform*, Mainz 1988.

F. ZEVI (ed.), *Pompei 79*, Naples 1979.

F. ZEVI (ed.), *Pompei, I-II*, Naples 1979.

Funerary statue
Late 1st cent. B.C.
Cemetery, Via Nucerina, Pompeii.

Printed in Italy by ILG LITOSTAMPA - Gorle